Lovecraft Laughing
Uncanny Memes in the Weird

Pál Hegyi

Lovecraft Laughing
Uncanny Memes in the Weird

Pál Hegyi

ⓒ 2019 Szeged, AMERICANA eBooks

General editors: Réka M. Cristian & Zoltán Dragon

ⓒ Pál Hegyi

ISBN: 978-615-5423-56-7 (.mobi); 978-615-5423-55-0 (.epub);
978-615-5423-54-3 (PoD)

Cover design: György Mézi Ács
Language editor: Shay Flanagan
Book design: Zoltán Dragon

AMERICANA eBooks is a division of *AMERICANA – E-Journal of American Studies in Hungary*, published by the Department of American Studies, University of Szeged, Hungary.
http://ebooks.americanaejournal.hu

ⓒ creative commons
This book is released under the Creative Commons 3.0 – Attribution – NonCommercial – NoDerivs 3.0 (CC BY-NC-ND 3.0) licene. For more information, visit: http://creativecommons.org/licenses/by-nc-nd/3.0/deed.hu

TABLE OF CONTENTS

What Do We Read When We Don't?	2
I. To Infinity and Beyond...	7
It is uncanny! – Memes, Theory, and Genres	9
Being of Two Minds	11
Out of Time – Repetition and Atemporality	14
II. Hunting Memes of 2 and 3 for Lack of a Haunting 1	18

    i. The **Doppelgänger** in E. A. Poe's "William Wilson" (proto-horror), H. P. Lovecraft's "The Dunwich Horror" and "The Outsider" (the weird), John Carpenter's *Prince of Darkness* (meme in genre transmutation)   19

    ii. The **Haunted House** as an *unheimlich*, mirroring, *mise-en-abymic* place in Shirley Jackson's "The Visit" (proto-horror), H. P. Lovecraft's "The Dreams in the Witch House" and "The Case of Charles Dexter Ward" (the weird), Roger Corman's *The Haunted Palace* (meme in genre transmutation)   22

    iii. The **Automaton** in Ambrose Bierce's "The Death of Halpin Frayser" and Henry James's "Sir Edmund Orme" (proto-horror), H. P. Lovecraft's "The Whisperer in Darkness" (the weird), Ridley Scott's *Alien* (meme in genre transmutation)   28

    iv. **Chance** and **Uncanny Coincidences** in William Fryer Harvey's "August Heat" (proto-horror), H. P. Lovecraft's "The Shadow Out of Time" and "The Temple" (the weird), Frank Darabont's *The Mist* (meme in genre transmutation)   33

    v. **Madness** and **Atemporality** in Charlotte Perkins Gilman's "The Yellow Wall-Paper" and Ambrose Bierce's "An Occurrence at Owl Creek Bridge" (proto-horror), H. P. Lovecraft's "At the Mountains of Madness" (the weird), John Carpenter's *In the Mouth of Madness* (meme in genre transmutation)   37

    vi. **Humor** as uncanny incongruity in Herman Melville's "The Lightning-Rod Man" and Mark Twain's "Chapter XIII" from *A Tramp Abroad* (proto-horror), H. P. Lovecraft's "In Defense of Dagon" (the weird), Henry Saine's *The Last Lovecraft: Relic of Cthulhu*, Stuart Gordon's *Re-Animator*, and Sam Mendes's *American Beauty* (memes in genre transmutation)   44

III. Evil Lives (and is Crossing Over)!	51
Works Cited	54

LOVECRAFT LAUGHING

UNCANNY MEMES IN THE WEIRD

> "The most merciful thing in the world, I think, is the inability of the human mind to correlate all its contents. We live on a placid island of ignorance in the midst of black seas of infinity, and it was not meant that we should voyage far. The sciences, each straining in its own direction, have hitherto harmed us little; but some day the piecing together of dissociated knowledge will open up such terrifying vistas of reality, and of our frightful position therein, that we shall either go mad from the revelation or flee from the deadly light into the peace and safety of a new dark age."
>
> H. P. Lovecraft

WHAT DO WE READ WHEN WE DON'T?

Popular culture is saturated with memes. Movies, comics, role-playing and computer games, and yes, even books showcase mutations spreading virally from a mutually shared cultural genome. We read them, listen to them, play them, watch them, copy-paste them, devour them. When discussing horror fiction, yet another question precedes the one present in the title of this introduction. What do we read in horror stories? To answer these persistent questions, research both historic and theoretical in nature is necessary. A comparison between proto-horror fiction by highly canonized nineteenth-century, early twentieth-century American authors and Lovecraftian poetics will reveal the presence of a theoretical thread that sutures these seemingly disparate literatures together. Classic short stories that are practically evergreens in undergraduate American literary history courses show a strikingly similar memetic conformation to what will be highlighted in works of weird fiction and the horror genre in general. Cthulhu's tentacles crawl out of the most unexpected corners of cinematography and literature, but the deity himself rarely appears in adaptations. It is more the likes of Stephen King's Pennywise the Clown who are hailed as the men of the hour. It is not without reason that King took the responsibility to author the introduction to the complete and unabridged edition of Howard Phillips Lovecraft's work. It is a gesture of gratitude, a token of appreciation and thankfulness for the building blocks of a textual universe that has since become the natural habitat for writers of the uncanny. By interpreting Lovecraftian fiction as a treasure trove of memes, a historic-theoretical survey will cast spotlight on six formative elements. Imported from the German, Italian, English, and Arabic idioms of literature to the new world during the nineteenth century, such tropes of the uncanny are being reconstructed and enriched by a large number of literary successors in a textual universe where, paradoxically, originality and recognition of copyrights are of essence. Identifying the memetic transmutations that the Freudian *Unheimlich* goes through in various close readings will offer a taxonomy of tropes as allegorizations of singularities, doubles, and triads. Such categorization applied to the weird genre unravels the poetics that is seen as an innately subversive impulse in literature.

The disruptive force of the uncanny can be attributed to an asymmetric polarity inherent in the term. As Freud insists, "The Uncanny (das *Unheimliche*, 'the unhomely') is in some way a species of the familiar (das

Heimliche, 'the homely')" (134). The uncanny phenomenology that results from such paradox will be expounded in sections discussing (i) the uncanniness of doublegoers; (ii) homely as both ugly and unhomely in mirrored, haunted places and *mise-en-abymes* (André Gide's literary term will be explicated here in detail); (iii) the uncanny as automaton; (iv) uncanny coincidences, chance events; (v) the uncanny sensation of perception connecting madness with a paradoxical concept of time; (vi) the uncanny effect of rhyming incongruities in humor. Each of the above sections will be introduced with a citation from Freud's seminal essay to highlight those textual places that implicitly create a taxonomy for memes of the uncanny. The stylistic consequences of Lovecraftian poetics propelled forward by the discursive forces in these memes will also be accounted for in filmic permutations and appropriations (as opposed to adaptations) utilizing the author's text.

A historic comparison will be conducted in analyses by a most diverse array of highly canonized American authors ranging from Edgar Allan Poe, Shirley Jackson, Ambrose Bierce, Henry James, William Fryer Harvey, through Charlotte Perkins Gilman, Herman Melville, and Mark Twain leading inevitably to Howard Phillips Lovecraft himself as progenitor and inexhaustible source of memetic inspiration for both his contemporaries and successors.

As seen from the above, within the field of the present investigation lie a scattered multitude of focal points. No matter how inefficient the economy of such a methodology may seem, the very reason for it is rooted in the subject matter of the exploration itself. For even making a reference to the genre to be examined here already poses a riddle. The literary works produced by a fuzzy set of canonized authors ranging from H. P. Lovecraft to China Miéville are labelled diversely as uncanny literature, horror stories, the gothic, the fantastique, the grotesque, supernatural fiction, and macabre among other variations. To mitigate the problem of denoting such a protean genre, the present work deliberately chose Lovecraft and Miéville as opposite ends of a temporal scale arching over a century. What links these two authors is their propensity to rely on the term "the weird tale" or in the latter case "the new weird" (Vandermeer and Vandermeer x), labels, which are well-known and widely accepted. Both "weird" as a term coined in the first decades of the twentieth century and its return a hundred years later can be characterized by a distinct blurring and blending of literary conventions. Crossing and breaking down genre boundaries, subverting clichés, and confronting readerly expectations are widely associated with the concept. "The weird" as an adjective promoted to substantival status will be used for two purposes. The first one is a technical consideration; it is of practical use for the object of this paper to differentiate between a Freudian theory of the uncanny and the weird as a term identifying a genre (i.e., uncanny literature). Secondly, the weird is seen as an appropriate concept to emphasize the radical dislocation innate in a particular type of narratives referred to with several other aforementioned and frequently used labels.

Since giving courses on popular culture in present-day academia seems more of a practice that created a norm rather than one provoking ongoing disputes on cultural hierarchies, when addressing the inherently subversive nature of the genre, this investigation turns to highly canonized authors. Late nineteenth- and early twentieth-century American writers occupy a distinguished place in literary history not only because of their artistic merits, but also due to their unique historical position. At the time, constructing a particularly American cultural identity went hand in hand with a competing effort to create a tradition that could be measured on a par with what hundreds of years had accumulated for their European rivals in the international arena. In this most inspiring and creative cultural context it was not the rare case that authors delved into the multifarious possibilities offered by different genres. It will be argued for that the inherently subversive puritan heritage, the unceasing dialogue between the legacy of transcendentalism and rationalist tenets that informed most of the *oeuvre*s of highly canonized authors is also responsible for prompting the recurrent emergence of the weird in literature.

Surveying the formative years of the late nineteenth, early twentieth century in American literature, one arrives at the conclusion that the *oeuvre* of authors now canonized as classics of high literature shows traits of a subversive kind. Puritan cultural heritage with its strong propensity toward dissent and nonconformity proffered a context with multiple accesses to genres in the popular register. Poe's balloon hoax of 1844 as a prefiguration of Orson Welless' *The War of the Worlds* broadcast in 1938 (based on a novel by H. G. Wells) provides a conspicuous example of how high and low registers melted into one in a literary epoch, when a uniquely and particularly American cultural identity was still under construction. A body of texts emerging in the span of a few decades around the *fin de siècle* can be interpreted, in retrospect, as instances of "proto-horror fiction" probing into territories seemingly outside the scope of critically accepted genre conventions. Mark Twain's *A Connecticut Yankee in King Arthur's Court* (1889) is one of the numerous illustrations of an innovative admixture of generic attributes creating a narrative that verges on, in this particular case, both the burlesque and speculative fiction. The ensuing six subsections of this paper set out to create parallels and comparisons between particular short stories by H. P. Lovecraft and "proto-horror" stories, as it were, by pre-eminent authors prolific around the turn of the century. The latter selection is based on the single criterion that these highly canonized authors have composed narrative forms that encompass the uncanny as a decisive element in their poetics. Close readings and case studies will be conducted in order to cast spotlight on prevalent memes interpreted as allegorizations of the uncanny, all of which already catalogued (and referenced in the titles by their respective page numbers) in Sigmund Freud's instructive essay written in 1919. Finally, at the end of each of the sections, the memetic nature of these tropes will be corroborated and showcased in filmic mutations (as opposed to adaptations) of the apparently ubiquitous Lovecraftian weird memes.

A historical inquiry of the subject matter leads inevitably to theoretical considerations as well. Before introducing a memetic approach to unravel parallels and similarities between the old and the new weird, it is necessary to give a brief account of some of the most productive theoretical advances toward an understanding of these genre formations.

The formalistic approach informing the work of Tzvetan Todorov (1971) has been passed on as one of the most influential and domineering traditions in contemporary criticism on the weird. Hesitation between the real vs. unreal and opposing familiar and unfamiliar states, the uncertainty between the natural and the supernatural are recurring elements when present-day scholars, for instance, Alice Mills attempts at defining the weird as an aesthetic quality in intermedial studies (53). Roger Luckhurst invites reception theory into dialogue when insisting that the new weird—the coinage of which term he attributes to M. John Harrison—emerged from the enthrallment of the audience. According to Luckhurst, such awe is induced by the vast terrain of possibilities that genre-crossings and the estranging capacity of the grotesque create for the readers (240). Noys and Murphy also rely on reception theory when they deploy the concept of hybrid structures in their comparison of the old and new weird and come to the conclusion that "central to attempts to define the weird as a genre has been its estrangement of our sense of reality" (118). Interaction studies attribute the success of the new genre to the emergence of subgroups or geek audiences who seek fringe experience (Mangan 197), while Miéville himself takes a post-Marxist standpoint in "Marxism and Fantasy: An Introduction" by contending that the fantastic mode "mimics 'the absurdity' of capitalist reality" (337). As will be discussed in the ensuing sections, psychoanalytic interpretations of the weird center on the repressed as the impossibility of enunciation. To add one another theoretical school to this list, Kate Marshall is an example for those scholars who draw on myth criticism describing the old weird as a genre built around the supernatural with "twisted mythic underpinnings" (631). A representative of narratology and genre studies, Spaulding concentrates on fissure in narratives of the weird insisting that "the supernatural appears as a rupture of the coherent universe" (79). Andrew Bennett and Nicholas Royle in chapters on the uncanny and the pleasure of reading predicate their statement on deconstructionism. In their text the weird as "a disturbance of the familiar" (34) intertwines with the concept of the "split subject who simultaneously enjoys, through the text, the consistency of its selfhood and its collapse" (197). As for the dialogue between Miéville and Lovecraft, critics and practitioners of the weird, both writers tie genre expectations to a sense of doubt, dread, and wonder. The former highlights "awe, and its undermining of the quotidian" (*Weird Fiction* 510) as the core element, while his predecessor states that "[a] certain atmosphere of breathless and unexplainable dread of outer, unknown forces must be present; and there must be a hint (…) of chaos and the dæmons of unplumbed space" (15).

Based on the above, "Gothic ambiguity" (*The Encyclopedia of The Gothic* 15) might seem a term empirical, appropriate and practical enough to include the various types of border-crossings that is detectable in the weird. Yet, any comprehensive categorization of cultural production and consumption is inexorably preceded by theoretical considerations, which, in their turn, create a foundation for the practice of identifying movements and new genres stemming from observable innovations in reading and writing.

The overwhelming output by such theoreticians as Tzvetan Todorov (1971), Gérard Genette (1979), Jacques Derrida (1980), and Hans Robert Jauss (1982) unraveled the paradoxical nature of the genre in general, yet it is a writer, Michel Houellebecq, whose anecdote gives a most illuminating commentary on the weird genre in particular. In his compelling book, *H. P. Lovecraft—Against the World, Against Life,* Houellebecq recounts that in the course of book-signings young enthusiasts asked him to sign his volume on Lovecraft not because they have read anything by the American author, but solely because they discovered "Lovecraft" through the intermediary of role-playing sessions or computer games (*Trail of Cthulhu*).

> At book signings, once in a while, young people come to see me and ask me to sign this book. They have discovered Lovecraft through role-playing games or CD-ROMs. They have not read his work and don't even intend to do so. Nonetheless, oddly, they want to find out more—*beyond the texts*—about the individual and about how he constructed his world. [emphasis added] (24-25)

Houellebecq's anecdote poses the question of what it is exactly that these young enthusiasts have actually discovered if not the narrations themselves. To answer, this investigation has to delineate what lies in the intersection of dominant genre definitions..

I. TO INFINITY AND BEYOND...

> "Look at me—listen to what I say—do you suppose there are really any such things as time and magnitude? Do you fancy there are such things as form or matter? I tell you, I have struck depths that your little brain can't picture! I have seen beyond the bounds of infinity and drawn down daemons from the stars... I have harnessed the shadows that stride from world to world to sow death and madness..."
>
> H. P. Lovecraft

The question raised by Houellebecq's is in essence a theoretical one to the extent that it directs toward further interrogations into genre definitions. The crux of the argument expounded by scholars lies in the fact that the genre displays a consequential resistance to be defined as a genre *per se*. The originality of any genre is addressed and scrutinized by Jauss's reception theory, where it is explicated that the operational functionality of the aesthetic category is dependent on repetition of elements in genre conventions to satisfy the requirements of generic expectations (23). Noys and Murphy cite Borges to disclose a similar pattern. "The fact is every writer creates his own precursors. His work modifies our conception of the past, as it will modify the future" (120). This continuous back and forth interaction between past and present canons makes it impossible to point to a moment of origin, to identify any first text that created genre conventions. Since it is not the seminal act of creation that animates a genre, but rather the inexhaustible process of resuscitation, "[t]he new text evokes for the reader (listener) the horizon of expectations and rules familiar from earlier texts, which are then varied, corrected, altered, or even just reproduced. Variation and correction determine the scope [...]" (Ibid.). With no detectable point of origin, genre as a question posed by a horizon of expectations is continuously under construction in the answers offered by particular works of art, which, in their turn, modify the proposition. This concept of the inherently memetic nature of all genres is corroborated by Derrida when he writes: "Suppose for a moment that it were impossible not to mix genres. What if there were, lodged within the heart of the law itself, a law of impurity or a principle of contamination" (57)?

Consulting theories on specific genre definitions comes with the presupposition that the given metalanguage itself will be contaminated by certain cognitive patterns constitutional in the subject matter intrinsically. If we narrow down the focus of genre classification to weird fiction, besides the memetic, reciprocative nature of repetition present in all genre constructions, there appears another binary, which is particularly characteristic to Todorov's understanding of the uncanny. In his work on *The Fantastic*, Todorov gives a definition of the genre as a reaction on the readers' part to a certain hesitation between two frames of reference, which are mutually exclusive. "There is an uncanny phenomenon which we can explain in two fashions, by types of natural causes and supernatural causes. The possibility of a hesitation between the two creates the fantastic effect" (18). One enters the marvelous if the laws of nature have to be transformed to account for supernatural phenomena. Yet, if the fantastic elements in the story are perceived in a way that the concept of reality is not seen by readers as altered, the narrative belongs to uncanny literature (31). The fantastic effect as an uncanny phenomenon is thus described by Todorov as a hesitation between the unreal and the real, the duration of uncertainty in perception. Consequently, the uncanny phenomenon, which is a main category, contains not only marvelous literature as one of its subcategories, but also uncanny fiction as a counterpart and a subordinate category. The cognitive pattern in the uncanny phenomenon that contaminated the metalanguage that is deployed to outline the generic structure of the uncanny could be visualized in the following Venn diagram:

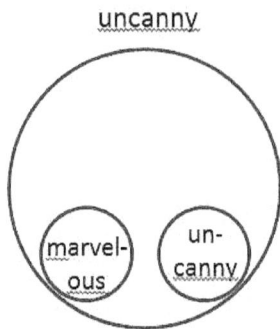

Since uncanny fiction is centered around continuous, radical dislocation *per se*, moving away from these expectations is a compulsion and an impossibility at the same time. The proliferation of genre mutations is made compulsive by the impossibility of pointing back to a single originary genre formation. The instability of the genre lies in its imitations, the memetic mutations of *unheimlich* phenomena. Todorov insists that the boundaries of this genre are marked by the extent and the limits of a hesitation between the imaginary and the real (17). Here the source of the uncanny affect is interpreted as the duration of uncertainty in perception, which hesitation is shifted to language and meaning through the chaotic madness of signification by the destabilizing forces of the uncanny. Todorov quotes Roger Callois with reference to infinite images, which "seek incoherence as a principle and reject any signification" (24). An effect of regression and progression *ad infinitum* is created by the asymmetry of Todorov's categorization summarized above in a *mise-en-abymic* diagram. A category which contains itself as its own subcategory opens up to both outward and inward mirroring surfaces. The uncanny phenomenon as the main category is divided into two genre categories (18), one of which is the uncanny genre, which, in turn, is characterized by the uncanny phenomenon being made up by two subordinate categories including the uncanny, which is then divided into another binary *ad infinitum*. The act of reception lodged in detective stories holds a similar potential to metafiction that the semantics of the uncanny in weird tales create for psychological horror. If the crime narrative—eminently in its surfictional mutations—generates self-referential texts about the impossibility of reading, the weird produces autopoetic tales about the impossibility of telling a story.

IT IS UNCANNY! – MEMES, THEORY, AND GENRES

> "The Thing cannot be described—there is no language for such abysms of shrieking and immemorial lunacy, such eldritch contradictions of all matter, force, and cosmic order."
>
> H. P. Lovecraft

In his 1919 essay, Freud, relying on Friedrich Wilhelm Joseph von Schelling's and Ernst Jentsch's work, sets out to delineate the nature of the uncanny by assembling what "evokes in us a sense of the uncanny" (124). What we receive is a taxonomy for the allegorizations or phenomena of a similar duality in the psyche, language, and signification. The nominalization of *das Unheimliche* already displays such dynamics between binaries in describing something that is un-homely, un-secretly, "the notion of the hidden and the dangerous" (134) which is to resurface. Yet, this binary is tripartite in the sense that it involves (1) the act of hiding something that remains to be (2) hidden for a period of time before it poses a danger to (3) reemerge. The self-propelling movement from a binary to a triad is an inevitable drift from a reassuring and symmetric duality of outward and inward realities toward the threat of a self-contained circular return within a three-element system. The asymmetry is strengthened by Freud's comment stating that "*Heimlich* thus becomes increasingly ambivalent, until it finally merges with its antonym *unheimlich*. The uncanny is in some way a species of the familiar (*das Heimliche*, 'the homely') (Ibid.)." The paradox is even more obvious in *The Standard Edition of the Complete Psychological Works of Sigmund Freud*, where James Strachey translates the same sentence with the following words: "*Unheimlich* is in some way or other a *sub-species* of Heimlich" [emphasis added] (225). *Unheimlich* is usually translated into English as "unhomely," yet "unsecretly" would be a more precise calque translation of the term. It also brings an understanding of the triality innate in this word closer. A secret place (as the familiarity of home) is a retreat from a state of being exposed, thus it already contains a movement of dislocation from anterior, threatening surroundings. Being unsecretly is not only a return to this condition, but a never-ceasing motion multiplied by progressive relations to the absent secret locality. Since Freud contends that due to its inherent ambivalence, *heimlich* merges with its antonym, the hierarchical relation between *unheimlich* (as a species of *heimlich*) can be summed in the diagram below. A sense of danger is what lies in the asymmetric structure of *unheimlich* as a category containing itself as a subcategory (134).

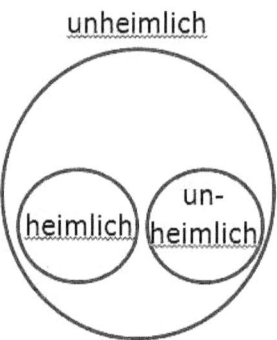

Freud refers to his findings interpreting the nature of the uncanny as "hints" (Ibid.), which is an indication of a signified never to be denoted by any signifiers but only indexed, implied as lack or a duration of "uncertainty" (139). This hesitation is associated with an allegorization of signification, where it is impossible to create a direct, denotative translation from sign to meaning (135). The uncanny narrative will be a representation of the trauma of not being able to tell a story that is always hiding somewhere else. Freud goes on to create a taxonomy of allegorical tropes, literary devices of duality (as displacements toward triads) that convey a sense of uncanniness. In the evolution of the ego from the singularity of primitive narcissism toward a multilayered self, Freud insists, the super-ego, which performs functions for self-consciousness becomes isolated, split off from the ego. "The double is a creation that belongs to a primitive phase in our mental development, a phase that we have surmounted, in which it admittedly had a more benign significance. The double has become an object of terror, just as gods become demons after the collapse of their cult" (143). Otto Rank makes a similar observation in "The Double" when, with a reference to Ernst Ludwig Rochholz, he states that guardian spirits had originally benevolent significance and "only gradually did their harmful (death) meaning develop along with the strengthening of the belief in a life after death" (51).

Being of Two Minds

> "But the moment of silence was broken—the surgings were speaking to him in a language that was not of physical sound or articulate words. 'The man of Truth is beyond good and evil,' intoned a voice that was not a voice. 'The man of Truth has ridden to All-Is-One. The man of Truth has learnt that Illusion is the only reality, and that substance is an impostor.'"
>
> H. P. Lovecraft

To expound the "benign significance" of dualities preceding the threat of triads, Julian Jaynes's popular theory on the bicameral mind ought to be utilized. Jaynes centers his work around the hypothesized former existence of static, sustained duality in any structure of identity. This premise is worth addressing for the same reason it was doomed to be falsified from the moment it was concocted. In his book of rather speculative nature, the American psychologist extrapolates a transitory process only to transform it into a permanent state. The utterly hypothetical nature of this scholarly endeavor lies in its regressive attempt at reducing the inherently triadic conformation of the psyche into a reassuring duality. Forming his proposition, Jaynes argues that some 3000 years ago the human brain was bi-chambered in its anatomy and cognitive structure as well with the right hemisphere giving orders to the left one, which perceived these commands as instructions coming from an external source as the voice of a god. No matter how heavily this theory has been debated since the 1970's, it still holds an appeal to a wide contemporary audience for the same reason it was denounced. Jaynes's concept is more of an idea belonging to the realm of science fiction than a scientific postulate. It is not by chance that the fiction of the bi-chambered consciousness has been utilized as the predominant feature of artificial intelligence in the speculative television series *West World*. As underscored above, it transforms a transitory state—Freud's premise on the body and its double as an immortal soul (142)—into a permanent condition of duality, a reassuring oscillation between the outside and the inside. Jaynes summarizes his hypothetical proposition for a symmetrical duality in human consciousness in the following lines: "In the bicameral era, the bicameral mind was the social control, not fear or repression or even law. There were [...] no private frustrations [...], since bicameral men had no internal 'space' in which to be private, and no analog to be private with" (205).Yet, it is precisely this comforting oscillation between an isolated outwardly superimposed reality and a secured inside subjugation that presents itself as the third element in the system, thus destabilizing the duality.

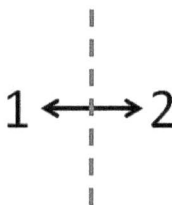

The multiplied layering of the ego is interpreted by Freud as a direct result of the fissure, split, chasm in binaries. Allegorizations of the uncanny (such as the *Doppelgänger*) can be both described as static (a stance in the lack of the homely, secretly) and dynamic. The latter characteristic as a compulsive return to that lack is also corroborated by the Greek etymology of tropes as movements or rather turns. In other words, the temporality of these allegorical tropes are stative in their dynamic repetitions or oscillations. A compulsion to repeat is explained as the uncanny affect by Freud, who, as mentioned before, argues that primitive narcissism created the first double of the body representing an "immortal" soul (142). Yet, Freud continues, as this doubled boundless self-love shifts towards the threefold structure in the (1) id, (2) ego, and (3) super-ego, "the double changes: having once been an assurance of immortality, it becomes the uncanny harbinger of death" (Ibid.). The double as an object of terror performs a regression to the singularity and oneness in a state, when and where the (1) ego is not established in opposition to (2) the other. In the diagram below, relying on Freud's first and second topographic models of personality, the central numeral 1 stands for the lack in the unconscious, while the other 1 on the left signifies the hinting, implying preconscious, which combined with the previous level creates the subconscious, whereas number 2 indexes the ego, and 3 stands for the superego.

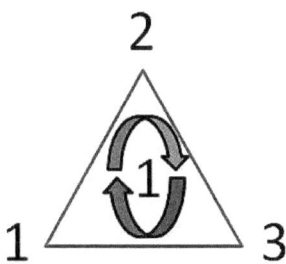

The "omnipotence of thought" in the animistic vestiges at the earliest phase of psychic development is expressed as a frightening, repressed element to which signification inevitably returns (Freud 147). The journey in this return creates a blurred territory between the fantastic and the real where the element of terror, which connects the mutually replaceable points of departure and destination, is turned—allegorized—into the uncanny. The signification process that governs meaning production in this territory of radical dislocation is both atemporal and simultaneous in nature. To shed light on the threateningly chaotic semiotics in such allegorizations of the uncanny as madness, chance events and atemporality, the argumentation must draw upon the psychological concepts *aléa* and synchronicity formulated by Michel Foucault and Carl Gustav Jung respectively. In his inaugural lecture at the Collège de France in 1970, Foucault determines chance (*aléa*) as a governing force in "discontinuous systematicities" "outside of the philosophies of the subject and of time":

> Furthermore, if discursive events must be treated along the lines of homogenous series which, however, are discontinuous in relation to each other, what status must be given to this discontinuity? It is of course not a matter of succession of instants in time, nor of the plurality of different thinking subjects. It is a question of ceasurae which break up the instant and disperse the subject into a plurality of possible positions and functions. This kind of discontinuity strikes and invalidates the smallest units that were traditionally recognised and which are the hardest to contest: the instant and the subject. [...] Finally, though it is true that these discontinuous discursive series each have, within certain limits, their regularity, *it is undoubtedly no longer*

possible to establish links of mechanical causality or of ideal necessity between the elements which constitute them. We must accept the introduction of the *aléa* as a category in the production of events. [emphasis added] ("The Order of Discourse" 63)

Meaningful coincidences with no causal relationship between them is what inform Jung's concept of synchronicity as well. "Jung used the word 'synchronicity' to characterize the significance of the simultaneity of events that could not be causally linked" (IX). Atemporality, the lack of causality is central to Jung when expounding his coined term:

> [S]ince experience has shown that under certain conditions space and time can be reduced almost to zero, causality disappears along with them, because causality is bound up with the existence of space and time and physical changes, and consists essentially in the succession of cause and effect. For this reason synchronistic phenomena cannot in principle be associated with any conceptions of causality. Hence the interconnection of meaningfully coincident factors must necessarily be thought of as acausal. (30)

When unraveling modes of uncanny signification in tropes of the uncanny in the ensuing sections, the argumentation of this work will inevitably return to acausal and atemporal incongruities. In the absence of one singular meaning, the co-occurrence of two or more disparate, dislocated elements on a homogenous, blurred narrative plane will result in a proliferation of signifying processes that are generated and made compulsive by the lack itself.

OUT OF TIME – REPETITION AND ATEMPORALITY

> "Time, the waves went on, is motionless, and without beginning or end. That it has motion, and is the cause of change, is an illusion. Indeed, it is itself really an illusion, for except to the narrow sight of beings in limited dimensions there are no such things as past, present, and future. Men think of time only because of what they call change, yet that too is illusion. All that was, and is, and is to be, exists simultaneously."
>
> H. P. Lovecraft

Jacques Lacan's corollary to Freud's theory in the *Four Fundamental Concepts of Psychoanalysis* and *Anxiety* emphasizes how the uncanny presents itself as an originary paradox in signification. The repetition compulsion, which has the power to override the pleasure principle by crossing all possible cognition, leads to a signal of the real as an inaccessible traumatic lacuna that is irreducible to any sign. The automaton as a chance for objects, as an insistence of signs, occupies a nontemporal locus between perception and consciousness (*Book XI* 56). Paul deMan also emphasizes the element of repetition regarding allegorical tropes in "The Rhetoric of Temporality":

> [I]t remains necessary, if there is to be allegory, that the allegorical sign refer to another sign that precedes it. The meaning constituted by the allegorical sign can then consist only in the *repetition* [...] of a previous sign with which it can never coincide, since it is of the essence of this previous sign to be pure anteriority" [emphasis added] (207).

The uncanny takes the place of representation, that—instead of signifying the real as absence—creates a doubled plane of signification to perform denotative gestures devoid of their signifying functions. The language of the uncanny is a ghostly allegory for signification with a tenor that precedes signs, which can only be hinted at or implied. Thus, the vehicle monopolizes its counterpart, that is, the tenor through a metaleptic shift from subcategory to category, from vehicle to a catachrestic allegory.

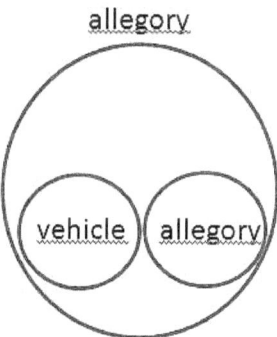

In a previous quotation by Freud *das Unheimliche* was defined as not a counterpart, but superimposed to *das Heimliche* (134). This asymmetry results in a proliferation of signifiers, which can be described as a recurring movement around the instability of signification. In what Lacan calls a "subjectifying homeostasis" it is not the denotative function but the dynamics created by the network of signifiers woven around the trauma that produces meaning (*Book XI* 55). Attribution of meaning gives way to a semantic performance on the impossibility of telling a story that is always somewhere else. The trauma of the inaccessibility of a singularity is performed in doubles and triads as allegorizations of the uncanny. These allegorizations are already enlisted in the taxonomy unfolding within the 1919 essay by Freud, who himself makes a peculiar reference to Mark Twain's *A Tramp Abroad* (144). Freud's memes of the uncanny will be interpreted in the works of highly canonized American authors. The period of the late nineteenth century, early twentieth century occupies a unique place in American literature, when authors were struggling to create their *suis generis* cultural identity in an international arena. This era of nativity and identity formation made this literature under construction susceptible to the singularities, dualities, and triads that are innate in identity constructions. During these formative years, many of the authors now revered as classical writers became invested in exploring allegorizations of the uncanny, which are associated with and integral to the conformation of the weird tale.

In the narratives to be analyzed bellow the singularity of the "unassimilable trauma" (Lacan, *Book XI* 55) will be performed in the interplay between doubles (and in several instances, triads), which concomitantly will create repetitive allegorical turns, circular movements of catachresis around the horror of the unspeakable. To quote Freud "[...] anything that can remind us of this inner compulsion to repeat is perceived as uncanny" (145). The allegorizations of the uncanny (in this essay interpreted as a radically subversive impetus in literature) are identified in Freud's instrumental essay with the *Doppelgänger*, the *unheimlich*, the Haunted house as an *unheimlich*, mirrored, *mise-en-abymic* place, the Automaton (the *prosopopeia* in ventrilloquist or puppet master vs. puppet), Chance events (Jung's synchronicity, Foucault's *aléa*), Madness, Atemporality, and weirdly enough: Humor. The itinerary will touch upon the following stations:

i. the **Doppelgänger**

> in "William Wilson" by E. A. Poe vs. "The Dunwich Horror," "The Outsider" by P.H. Lovecraft; meme in genre transmutation: *Prince of Darkness*, 1987. Dir. by John Carpenter

ii. the **Haunted House** as an *unheimlich*, mirroring, *mise-en-abymic place*

> in "The Visit" by Shirley Jackson vs. "The Dreams in the Witch House" and "The Case of Charles Dexter Ward" by H. P. Lovecraft; meme in genre transmutation: *The Haunted Palace,* 1963. Dir. by Roger Corman

iii. the **Automaton**

> in "The Death of Halpin Frayser" by Ambrose Bierce, "Sir Edmund Orme" by Henry James vs. "The Whisperer in Darkness" by H. P. Lovecraft; meme in genre transmutation: *Alien,* 1979. Dir. by Ridley Scott

iv. **Chance** and **Uncanny Coincidences**

> in "August Heat" by William Fryer Harvey vs. "The Shadow Out of Time," "The Temple" by H. P. Lovecraft; meme in genre transmutation: *The Mist,* 2007. Dir. by Frank Darabont

v. **Madness**, **Atemporality**

> in "The Yellow Wall-Paper" by Charlotte Perkins Gilman, "An Occurrence at Owl Creek Bridge" vs. "At the Mountains of Madness" by H. P.; meme in genre transmutation: *In the Mouth of Madness,* 1994. Dir. by John Carpenter

vi. **Humor**

> in "The Lightning-Rod Man" by Herman Melville vs. "In Defense of Dagon" by H. P. Lovecraft, *A Tramp Abroad* (Chapter XIII) by Mark Twain; meme in genre transmutation: *The Last Lovecraft: Relic of Cthulhu,* 2009. Dir. by Henry Saine, *Re-Animator,* 1985. Dir. by Stuart Gordon, *American Beauty,* 1999. Dir. by Sam Mendes

II. HUNTING MEMES OF 2 AND 3 FOR LACK OF A HAUNTING 1

> "That is not dead which can eternal lie,
> And with strange aeons even death may die."
>
> H. P. Lovecraft

As the previous section argued, identifying a center in the genre definition of the weird is problematic because it is in the disseminating memetic mutations of the same tropes for dislocation (i.e., different allegorizations of the *Unheimlich*) where the loci of the genre can be determined. The narrative uncanniness of the weird arises from the tension between discursive strategies of repressing the other's story and its indirect manifestations in compulsive allegorical recourses. The signifieds are contained within a dissociated semantic field where they cannot be denoted, only referred to in allegorical narrativization. The tale becomes weird through its self-definition as a story about the impossibility of telling itself. The adjective "weird" is descriptive of form and contents at the same time. The split nature of a form uncannily signifying the content that is being created by the very uncanniness of that form results in a continuous movement towards prosopopoeial frames of references.

To shed light on the inherently memetic nature of the various allegorizations of Freud's *unheimlich*, one has to turn to genre permutations of these memes, movies, video and role-playing games (Petersen, Willis 1999), in one particular case even a rock opera (*Dreams in the Witch House: A Lovecraftian Rock Opera*, 2013). Filmic adaptations of Lovecraft's short stories and novels have never been particularly successful, out of over more than forty attempts only few have come close to what might be called critical or popular acclaim. "HPL's works are notoriously challenging to translate into films, which is one reason why truly outstanding pictures have been so rare in Lovecraft films" (Mitchell 7). It is rather a cultural evolution through replication that informs the memetic phenomenology in various genres as influence exerted exclusively by deploying formative elements in the Lovecraftian *oeuvre*. More of an inspiration than textual reference, Lovecraftian memes will be interpreted as underpinnings upon which such towering monuments have been erected as John Carpenter's *Apocalypse*

Trilogy, Ridley Scott's *Alien* franchise, or the popular role playing-game, *The Trail of Cthulhu* based on August Derleth's collection of short stories with the same title (1962), a literary mutation itself.

Definitions of memes may vary, but the works by leading authorities on the subject matter generally seem to agree that a meme is a cultural element that is transmitted by non-genetic means, yet in a manner analogous to the biological transmission and evolution of genes, that is, by imitation and repetition (Blackmore 8). These are mechanisms "via which cultural information can be preserved in a way that enables it to be replicated and to exert control over its effects in a variety of contexts" (Distin 34). The memetic conformation of the Lovecraftian universe of weird and uncanny tales is laid bare by the nativity of the Cthulhu myth itself. For instance, Tsathoggua was brought to life by Clark Ashton Smith's "The Tale of Satampra Zeiros" (written in 1929) but was first put in print by Lovecraft in "The Whisperer in Darkness" (only three months before Smith's story was published in 1931). The name of Hastur (The Unspeakable One, Him Who Is Not to be Named) first appeared in Ambrose Bierce's short story "Haïta the Shepherd" (1893), two years later was borrowed by Robert W. Chambers ("The Repairer of Reputations"), then by Lovecraft in "The Whisperer in Darkness" (1931), until finally it evolved into *The Hastur Cycle* compiled from the works of various authors in 1993. The Cthulhu mythos, which is an ever-expanding shared universe (e.g., *Call of Cthulhu* role-playing game) based on fragmented and scattered themes in short stories by Lovecraft, was first recognized and developed by August Derleth, who infamously billed himself as Lovecraft's posthumous collaborator.

In each of the subsections bellow, after having created parallels between short stories written by highly canonized American authors and those by H. P. Lovecraft, a movie interpreted as a memetic transmission of the given trope of the uncanny will also be included in the investigation to showcase one particular Lovecraftian meme.

i. The Doppelgänger

> One must content oneself with selecting the most prominent of those motifs that produce an uncanny effect [...] of the "double" (the *Doppelgänger*) [...], a person may identify himself with another and so become unsure of his true self; or he may substitute the other's self for his own. The self may thus be duplicated, divided and interchanged. Finally there is the constant recurrence of the same thing, the repetition of the same facial features, the same characters, the same destinies, the same misdeeds, even the same names, through successive generations. (Freud 141-142)

Edgar Allan Poe's "William Wilson" offers a textbook example for the inexhaustible aesthetic potential that lies within the conflict of the split self. Yet, the doubling is first introduced in a prefiguration for the William Wilson *Doppelgänger* in the externalized character of the Reverend Dr. Bransby. An authorative figure of a principal, John Barnsby's persona displays traits of a "double nature" having a countenance at times "demurely benign" and yet, on other occasions, a "sour visage" is observed by students (335). The building of the school itself, which is reminiscent of the infinite regresses and *mise-en-abymic* dimensions of *a pars pro toto* space of soul with "no end to its windings," is divided into "two stories" and attended by "two ushers" (336). These doubles are interiorized and regressed into the mirror images hidden behind the names of two William Willsons, twins who are confounded by "detestable coincidence", and separated merely by the third element, a connecting surface in oscillation, the spectral voice of the other, "a very low whisper" (340). In consequence, a gradual breakdown of the narrative plane is being performed within the triadic structure of the (1) unnamed narrator as a destructive force, (2) William Wilson as compunction personified in a separate identity, Freud's eternal soul, and the (3) voice, which regains its essence only in unifying death. Irrational fear, a gothic atmosphere of impending doom, a sense of inescapable imprisonment motivates the drama of the narrative. The innovation in poetics is created by the substitution of the conventional conflict between protagonist and antagonist with a compulsive insistence for the *Doppelgänger* to return to his double. This compelling will is embodied in the endless language games hidden in the rhyming pair of the mirroring names, the initial "double yous," the hidden capacity for language games: "will I am, will's on," "Will, I am Will's son". In the climax it is a destructive act of aggression and transgression, the irreducible collapse of the third element that inverts the polarity of host and parasite, thus replacing the ghost-like echo of the other with the voice of the narrator. The narrative of the homley, *heimlich* name, the originary secret of the story in the end is not possible to be told, rather it is the *unheimlich* horror of the double, the collapse of the opposition between the ego and the other that is presented as a sublime singularity by the closure of the plot.

A memetic variation of a similar conformation around an externalized double gradually shifting into an internal split is at work in H. P. Lovecraft's short story "The Dunwich Horror" as well. Here, it is a series of generational metalepses, a regression of geneological *mise-en-abymes* that creates a mirroring effect reflecting on the inadmissibility of an originary father. Wilbur Whateley's figure is portent with the same duality as the William Wilson character. The double nature of their names opens a gateway toward the singularity of an unknown, invisible, unassimilable trauma. In "Dunwich Horror," the transparency the albino mother in Lavinia—a counterpart for her "dark, goatish-looking infant"—creates the oscillating surface as a territory for the incessant movements between the *Doppelgänger* and the inaccessible unity of the traumatic locus (636). The farmhouse in the story incorporates boundless, immeasurable expanses indexing the soul as a system containing a bigger *pars pro toto* structure than itself. A compulsive return to a genealogical origin is paralleled with a proliferation of dualities. Whereas the plot line follows a pattern of continuous progression towards the possibility of alluding to the name of the unnamable originary singualrity in the father Yog-Sothoth, "double yous," and other rhyming alliterations contaminate the text. "Wilbur Whateley" (636), "witch Whateley" (640), the repeated moniker "Wizard Whateley's" (651, 652, 661, 667), the ever present "whippoorwills" (a word repeated twenty times on thirty-three pages), "Arkham Advertiser" (641), "Fred Farr" (659), these textual alliterations, doublings reach their dramatic peak with their collapse. The entire plotline revolves around duplicating hints towards the singularity of the unnamable father. In the climax of the narrative, the implosion of these dualities discloses the lacuna embedded in the text. As the copious number of alliterations imply, the dramatization of the unassimilable trauma is played out at a phonological level. The "W" splits into double "V"-s, then, losing essence, becomes unvoiced transforming into two "f"-s and ultimately, into one single consonant, the first letter in "Father" as the initial of the final referent: "*ff—ff—ff*—FATHER! Father! YOG-SHOTHOTH!..." (666). The irrevocable deconstruction of the narrative is swirling around the dead center of the paradoxical singularity in the name of the father: a name, which presents itself as a violent and contaminating textual intrusion by a narrative never to be told.

In the same vein, Poe's "William Wilson" is the dramatization of the inability and impossibility of uttering the name of the narrator. "Let me call myself, for the present, William Wilson. The fair page now lying before me need not be sullied with my real appellation. This has been already too much an object for the scorn, for the horror, for the detestation of my race" (330). The story that is not to be told unfolds in the singularity of the name behind the mask(s) of William Wilson. The narrative thus is nothing but an expression of its very effort to create a discursive condition when direct speech—addressing the self in the second person singular—becomes a possibility, even if at the expense of putting an end to an imploding plot. "In me didst thou exist—and, in my death, see by this image, which is thine own, how utterly though hast murdered thyself" (354).

Meme in genre transmutation

A memetic permutation of Lovecraft's doubles, *Prince of Darkness* (1987) directed by John Carpenter creates a parallel with just another short story on the author's *Doppelgänger*s, namely "The Outsider" (1921). Its plot, which is centered around the uncanny experience of recognizing an abject other in the mirror image, is unfolding in an *unheimlich* place, "a venerable ivied castle in a thickly wooded park; maddeningly familiar, yet full of perplexing strangeness to me" (167). The sublime climax both of the short story and the movie is the dramatic point when the protagonist's hand is touching the "*cold and unyielding surface of polished glass*" [emphasis in original] (169), at which moment these narratives collapse. The singular instance of a union with the "Anti-God" just as with the "Anti-Outsider" constitutes a whirling aporia, the place of the impossible. The narratives, which are direct expressions of the effort to allude to a story never to be told, generate an implosion. The poetics thus created radically differs from the schematic closure of horror stories, wherein the final scene portends that the evil seemingly subdued is still in our midst. Lacking the capacity to open up for incessant homogenous repetitions, the *Doppelgänger* as a meme reifying a search for unity in identification inevitably leads to the weird shock of ending all communication, to the dreadful death of the work of art itself.

ii. The **Haunted House** as an *unheimlich*, mirroring, *mise-en-abymic* place

> One would suppose, then, that the uncanny would always be an area in which a person was unsure of his way around: [...] ["an eerie place"] – *locus suspectus*; [...] (of a house): *haunted*. (Freud 125)

> To many people the acme of the uncanny is represented by anything to do with death, dead bodies, revenants, spirits and ghosts. Indeed, we have heard that in some modern languages the German phrase *ein unheirrdiches Haus* ['an uncanny house'] can be rendered only by the periphrasis "a haunted house." (148)

A heraldic concept in its origins, the *mise-en-abyme* as an emblem for regressive mirroring was first described by in Claude-Edmonde Magny's *Histoire du roman français depuis 1918*. In 1989, Lucien Dällenbach in his *The Mirror in the Text* reconstructed the *mise-en-abyme* as a theoretical concept into a narrative figure of intertextuality. Yet, it was Mieke Bal four years earlier, who, by suggesting an English translation for the French term in *Narratology*, cast spotlight on the uncanny doubling, mirroring nature of the concept:

> This phenomenon (the embedded text presenting a story that resembles the primary fabula) is comparable to infinite regress. In French the term is 'mise-en-abyme.' This term derives from heraldry, where the phenomenon occurs in pictorial representation. In literature, however, we have to do with infinite

regress in the medium of language. It would be wrong, therefore, to overstress the analogy to graphic representation, since in language mise-en-abyme occurs in a less 'ideal' form. What is put into the perspective of infinitive regress is not the totality of an image, but *only a part of the text*, or a certain aspect. To avoid needless complications, I suggest we use the term 'mirror-text' for 'mise-en-abyme.' [emphasis added] (57-58)

The concept of escutcheon as the shield within the shield displays a very similar asymmetric *pars pro toto* structure to the ones detected in the previous diagrams.

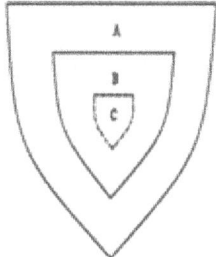

A mirroring, duplicating effect revealing itself in the uncanniness of a haunted place is exemplified in the new weird tale of *The City & The City* by China Miéville. Besźel and Ul Qoma are situated in the same geographical location separated by an invisible border. In this synchronicity, a secondary, mirroring world exists as a Foucauldian heterotopia ("Of Other Spaces, Heterotopias" 46-49), a place of utter otherness that subverts a hierarchical, preexisting source of origin for both these locations. The unity of the locus (1) is split into two reflective surfaces (2), which, in their turn, inevitably lead to the creating of the connecting surface (3) in this juxtaposition. In his *mise-en-abymic* book-within-the-book entitled *Between the City and the City*, doctor Bowden states that between the cities of Besźel and Ul Qoma a third one resides. The citizens of Orciny are believed to be invisible to residents of both the other cities. The way they dress and move makes it possible for these denizens to oscillate between the *The City & The City*. Miéville's novel itself becomes a *mise-en-abyme*, for it is structured in a tripartite fashion (with parts entitled (1) Besźel, (2) Ul Qoma, and (3) Breach) mirroring the overlapping threefold construct of the cities. This structure is best conceptualized in Benczik's elaboration on her innovatively coined term, the "spatial echo" (205). Benczik's term, incorporating a familiar territory and its spectral image along with the mirroring plane between them, is poignantly evocative of the myth of Narcissus and Echo, a mythotheme on the interminable regress of the originary self in infinity mirrors.

The City & The City as an acclaimed achievement in new weird fiction finds parallels for its deployment of uncanny, *mise-en-abymic* mirroring places not only in stories published in the early editions of *Weird Tales* but also in Shirley Jackson's "The Visit". In his biography entitled *Shirley Jackson's American Gothic*, Darryl Hattenhauer contends that Shirley Jackson was among the few proto-postmodernists to anticipate the paradigm shift from modernism to the ensuing episteme. He corroborates Jackson's canonic position by highlighting the fact that "[i]n 1968, Macmillan's Literary Heritage series included her with Edgar Allen Poe, Nathaniel Hawthorne, Herman Melville, Mark Twain, Henry James [...] in its canonical anthology *The American Experience: Fiction*" (1). Shirley Jackson first published her short story "A Visit" in 1950 under its original title "The Lovely House," the intricate text of which is woven of memetic fibers already intertwined in the imaginative fabrication of Lovecraft's work.

Just as the initial word of the short story is the noun phrase "the house," the first utterance of the protagonist also characterize the very same place as "It's a lovely house" (249). From a focalized point of view the reader is informed that Margaret "felt that she too had come *home*" [emphasis added] (Ibid.). The story shifts from this homely feeling at the start to the utter unhomeliness of the closure; from the temporality of a narrative to the timelessness of a frozen image as the story sets confronts a timeless unity with the temporal movement necessary to render meaning to the pieces of a fragmented entirety.

> She could see the fine threads of the weave, and the light colors, but *she could not have told the picture unless she went far away*, perhaps as far away as the staircase, and looked at it from there; perhaps, she thought, from halfway up the stairway this great hall, and perhaps the whole house, is visible, as a complete body of story together, all joined and in sequence. Or perhaps I shall be allowed to move slowly from one thing to another, observing each, or would that take all the time of my visit? [emphasis added] (Ibid.)

In the first section of the three-part story the beholder's eye moves across a pattern of tiles in the hall "too large to be seen from the floor" to first, the genealogical *mise-en-abyme* of the gold room: "mama"; "grandmamas"; "great-grandmamas"; "great-great grandmamas" (251), then secondly, to the irrationality of the silver room, which "shows the house in moonlight" (Ibid.). The inevitable remove from the immediate proximity of particularities in order to gain perspective opens up the third chamber of parallel, infinity mirrors, which project ever-diminishing reflections within a Chinese box: "another within that, and another within that one" (Ibid.). The oscillating, mirroring surface of this third room is what separates the cognizant rationality of the "sunlight" (Ibid.) in the gold room from the irrational whiteness of the silver one. The reason Margaret finds this third room frightening is because "it was so difficult to tell her what was in it and what was not" (252), whether the reassuring oscillation between the poles of a duality is extrapolated into the dynamics of a triad as depicted in the pictures describing the dynamics in twos and threes above. There is a compulsive effort palpable in the story to incorporate an external third element. "That evening Carla and Margaret played and sang duets, although Carla said that their voices together were too thin to be appealing without a deeper voice accompanying, and that when her brother came they should have some splendid trios" (254).

The ultimate trauma of the plot concerns the absence of the captain/brother *Doppelgänger*, the unassimilable lacuna to which the circular and regressive returns always fail. Two mirroring screens facing each other not only end up in (a) endless mirroring and (b) coincidences, but also in (d) inversions and (e) disappearances. Here are few of the countless examples: (a) the miniature mosaic replica made of the material from the house itself, within which Mrs. Montagues needlework depicting the building is in progress (255); (b) by "coincidence" (263) both the guest and the great-aunt are called Margaret; (c) while glimpsing her miniature representation in the tiles, Margaret asks: "What is *this*?" and then repeats "*What* is this?" [emphasis in original] (255); (e) when the captain/brother *Doppelgänger* disappears from the story, so does the single male first name that connected the doubles in their undecidability: "*and Paul?; Who was Paul?*" [emphasis in original] (273). The "lovely house" serves as an index for the self, a *mis-en-scéne* where the drama of performing the identity is played out. The noticeable cracks on the whole of the house cannot be repaired (270), aging components cannot be replaced. In the vortex of the *mise-en-abyme*, no action or movement in time is possible: "We shall be models of stillness," says Carla, laughing (273). Nothing can be changed or replaced in any of the mirror images: "All we can do is add to it" (273). By placing an extra set of figurines (automata) in the foreground of a new, multiplied layer within the *mise-en-abyme*, the horror of compulsive repetition is infinitively prolonged outside the dimension of time.

Meme in genre transmutation

It seems to be of common belief that Lovecraft's concept of and constant reference to non-Euclidean geometry was inspired by a lecture on the 9th of November in 1931 (Carlin, Allen 79). Yet, if one reads the text of the lecture entitled "The Size of the Universe" (de Sitter 89-104), it becomes obvious that—influential as the presentation must have been for an audience first introduced to the notion of the ever-expanding universe—it has nothing to do with geometry. What is certain, though, is that there are countless instances for haunted castles and non-Euclidean architectures in Lovecraft's fiction. Lovecraft himself, who dropped out of school numerously, does sound less than enthusiastic about geometry when he writes in his personal correspondence: "In studies I was not bad – except for mathematics, which repelled and exhausted me. I passed in these subjects – but just about that. Or rather it was algebra which formed the bugbear. Geometry was not so bad" ("To Robert" 170).

Euclidean geometry is a study of plane and solid geometry based on five axioms formed by the Greek mathematician Euclid (c. 300 BCE). It is a discipline all students in elementary and high schools are taught. The adjectives "plane" refers to the fact that geometric properties of the objects studied exist in a two-dimensional space. It is common knowledge that the shortest distance between two points is a straight line, also, that the he sum of the measures of the interior angles of a triangle is 180 degrees, and that parallel lines never cross. Objects such as triangles, circles, squares can be deemed into three-dimensional pyramids, spheres, and cubes extending plane geometry to the three-dimensional Euclidean space of solid geometry. The fifth, parallel axiom by Euclid postulates that if the sum of the measurement of two interior angles formed by two straight lines intersected by a third one is less than 180 degrees, these lines extended indefinitely will meet on the side where the sum is less than 180 degrees. To put it simply, if two lines are not parallel they cross on one side—where the sum is less than two tight angles— and become ever-distancing on the other. If the parallel axiom is replaced, two possible forms of alternative geometry arise: hyperbolic and elliptic geometries. János Bolyai published a 26 page long work with the title "Appendix" in 1831, in which the Hungarian mathematician "made a revolutionary achievement by the creation of the so-called non-Euclidean geometry" (Prékopa 3). In two dimensions, instead of a flat surface, objects in these geometries are in hyperbolic or elliptic planes. For instance, the sum of the interior angles of a hyperbolic triangle is always less than 180 degrees, whereas in the case of an elliptic one it is more than a straight angle. To visualize these hyperbolic (Bolyai 31) and elliptic (182) triangles, all one has to do is project a Euclidean triangle on the outer or the inner surface of a sphere respectively. If the given surfaces on which the triangles are placed could be laid out flat, in consequence the fifth axiom was reinstated and the sides of both triangles would run parallel in Euclidean geometry.

This digression was necessary not only to point out that Lovecraft's recurring "non-Euclidean geometry" is more than just a mysterious catchphrase, but also to underline that hyperbolic and elliptic curvatures of three-dimensional space are evocative of outer progression and inner regression towards otherworldly, ungraspable, unknowable dimensions in the Lovecraftian universe. As will be discussed in detail in the section on atemporality, vertiginous, paradoxical, non-Euclidean architectures and structures open up visual perception towards unfathomable measurements. Their *mise-en-abymic* attribute to propel the story towards the vanishing point of regressive mythologies run parallel with a seemingly endless chain of memetic signifiers. One of the most obvious illustrations to enlist here would be "The Case of Charles Dexter Ward" (1927), which is not only a memetic inspiration for ensuing works of art, but one that thrives on a tradition of memes itself. A most conspicuous allusion is offered by the ever-present "gables" (495, 496, 517, 524) an allusion to *The House of the Seven Gables* by Nathaniel Hawthorne, who Lovecraft praised as "New England's greatest contribution to weird literature" in his *Supernatural Horror in Literature* (64). "The Case of Charles Dexter Ward" was adapted to the big screen in 1963 as *The Haunted Palace* directed by Roger Corman. No matter how the plot bears semblance to even "The Shadow over Innsmouth" (1931), the movie was first released as *Edgar Allan Poe's The Haunted Palace* as reference to Poe's poem with the same title that Poe later incorporated in one of the most uncanny short stories on the *Doppelgänger* in world literature, "The Fall of the House of Usher."

Another conspicuous example for a house with unearthly geometry opening up to multiple dimensions is Lovecraft's "Dreams in the Witch House."

> Gilman's room was of good size but queerly irregular shape; [...] there was no access—nor any appearance of a former avenue of access—to the space which must have existed between the slanting wall and the straight outer wall on the house's north side [...]. The loft above the ceiling—which must have had a slanting floor—was likewise inaccessible. [...] Old Keziah, he reflected, might have had excellent reasons for living in a room with peculiar angles; for was it not through certain angles that she claimed to have gone outside the boundaries of the world of space we know? His interest gradually veered away from the unplumbed voids beyond the slanting surfaces, since it now appeared that the purpose of those surfaces concerned the side he was already on. (861)

Here, the inaccessible center of the *mise-en-abyme* is presented by the singularity of the ultimate horror, which is unknown, unexplainable, impossible to be told, only continuously hinted at over and over again in compulsive series of returns and approximations. No matter how many memetic transmutations are available now, comprehensive mythologies of Azathoth, Cthulhu, Dagon, Nyarlathotep, Tsathoggua, and Yog-Sothoth have only been crafted by Lovecraft's "posthumous collaborators." The mysterious Necronomicon or the Cthulhu myth had never been condensed into a coherent narrative in any of Lovecraft's work, *Tales of the Cthulhu Mythos* in 1998 was co-authored by fifteen different writers. The mythothemes remained fragmented hints in Lovecraft's writings for the simple reason that these narratives are halted by the inaccessible boundaries of the traumatic lacuna, the contours of which are made visible by the failing attempts to penetrate the core. As the author defines his genre in *Supernatural Horror in Literature*:

> The true weird tale has something more than secret murder, bloody bones, or a sheeted form clanking chains according to rule. A certain atmosphere of breathless and *unexplainable dread of outer, unknown* forces must be present; and there must be *a hint* (…) of chaos and the dæmons of unplumbed space. [emphasis added] (15)

Creating an atmosphere of "unexplainable dread" is paramount for any adaptations of Lovecraft's stories because ultimately these tales of the weird are a far cry from character- or end-driven narratives. Most adaptations fall prey to their own desire to tell a story, whereas Lovecraftian memes are utilized as building blocks creating an ambience of "cosmic horror" (25). In his poetics Lovecraft created an atmosphere portent with hints and allusions to the unspeakable story, an *unheimlich* context that renders the existence of humanity utterly insignificant. Dimension after dimension lead the protagonist deeper into the maelstrom of the unknown in "Dreams in the Witch House." "There were suggestions of the vague, twilight abysses, and of still vaster, blacker abysses beyond them—abysses in which all fixed suggestions of form were absent" (874).

Atmosphere, indeed, is what has been captured by the few successful and daring adaptations of Lovecraft's stories. The second television episode (*H. P. Lovecraft's Dreams in the Witch-House*) in the first season of *Masters of Horror* (2005-2007) proved to be a persuasive success with its gloomy tone, just as, despite expectations to the contrary, "Dreams in the Witch House: A Lovecraftian Rock Opera" as a musical plethora of foreboding premonitions turned out to be an eldritch transmutation of the Lovecraftian meme in 2014.

iii. The **Automaton**

According to Freud, who quotes Jentsch to support his argument, the automaton operates as the expression of the

> doubt as to whether an apparently animate object really is alive and, conversely, whether a lifeless object might not perhaps be animate […]. One of the surest devices for producing slightly uncanny effects through storytelling is to leave the reader wondering whether a particular figure is a real person or an automaton, and to do so in such a way that his attention is not focused directly on the uncertainty, lest he should be prompted to examine and settle the matter at once, for in this way, as we have said, the special emotional effect can easily be dissipated. (Jentsch qtd. in Freud 135)

In the above quotation the emphasis is yet again laid on the fact that employing any allegorization of the uncanny that is "focused directly on the uncertainty" is a mimetic act in the Platonic sense. To "settle the matter at once" is an indication to the lack of temporal aspect, which excludes the diegetic counterpart. An ambience of uncertainty is what is epitomized in John Carpenter's *The Thing* (1982), a film that is widely acclaimed as a direct reaction to, if not a quasi-adaptation of Lovecraftian memes, in this case, from Lovecraft's *At the Mountains of Madness*. Built less on a plot line progressing toward a resolution of mystery than one indulging in the undecidability between inanimate objects and humans, this movie shows the same principal characteristics of poetics that is detectable, among many others, in "The Whisperer in Darkness" written by Lovecraft in 1930. Yet, to unravel the intricate patterns generated by the binaries of plurality versus singularity, this paper will interpret one of the highly canonized short stories by Ambrose Bierce, who Lovecraft pays homage to in his *Supernatural Horror in Literature* (with a quote by Samuel Loveman) for an "uncannily precise" atmosphere (65). *The Death of Halpin Frayser* written in 1891 is particularly lauded here by Lovecraft citing F.T. Cooper, who asserts that it is "the most fiendishly ghastly tale in the literature of the Anglo-Saxon race" (Ibid.).

Ambrose Bierce's "The Death of Halpin Frayser" written in 1891 was particularly lauded by Lovecraft. The narrative revolves around a story not to be told, the unspeakable trauma of an incestuous, murderous relationship between mother and son. "The two were nearly inseparable, and by strangers observing their manner were not infrequently mistaken for lovers" (6). "There is some rascally mystery here," said Detective Jaralson adding "I hate anything of that kind" (15). Halpin Frayser's untainted identity preexists the plurality, multitude inherent in the triad of his split selves. First, Detective Jaralson hides Branscom behind the veil of a mistaken identity, that is, Pardee, until in the final revelation he identifies the murderer of Catherine Larue as Larue. It is the utterance of the mother's name that propels the narrative into motion in the opening paragraphs: "One dark night in midsummer a man waking from a dreamless sleep in a forest lifted his head from the earth, and staring a few moments into the blackness, said: 'Catherine Larue.' He said nothing more; no reason was known to him why he should have said so much" (1). The new identity of the mother—called "Katy" (5) by the loving son—presents a mystery, yet solving the riddle stops short at the precise moment when the name exposed in the title, the originary, singular identity of Halpin Frayser could be returned to. This identity that served as the protagonist for the tripartite dream sequence of the short story (section I, II, III) can only be implied and hinted at in section IV, which shrouds the aftermath of the dissemination of Halpin Frayser's self into a triad of selves in the disguise of a detective story. Here ratiocination serves as camouflage, which cloaks the traumatic singularity in the story: "'Larue,

Larue!"' exclaimed Holker, with sudden animation. 'Why, that is the real name of Branscom—not Pardee. And—bless my soul! how it all comes to me—the murdered woman's name had been Frayser'" (15)! The return to the name of Katy Frayser masked as Catherine Larue, which initiated the narrative, is both an allusion to and a diversion from the only name not possible to be uttered, that is, the name of Halpin Frayser.

The two Larues, Catherine and Halpin, as *Doppelgängers*, share the preexisting singularity of their inaccessible name in oblivion. The dream sequence sets out with a dreamless dream in section I., in which "staring a few moments into the blackness" (1), Halpin spoke "aloud a name that he had not in memory" (2). The trauma of matricide—later inverted into filicide at the end of section III.—is just as inassimilable: "he felt as one who has murdered in the dark, not knowing whom nor why" (3). The mechanical, self-activating plurality of "unintentional returns" (Freud 144) to a traumatic singularity is strengthened by a distinction between the essence of silence and inactivity (3, 8, 14, 15) and the multitude of sounds and voices: "an infinite multitude of unfamiliar sounds" (3), "a murmur of swarming voices" (8). A haunting genealogical *mise-en-abyme* in the poetic talent passed on from the maternal great-grandfather, Myron Bayne through Katy Frayser to Halpin Frayser also accentuates the effect of infinity in split selves. Yet, the most compelling aspect in the interpretation of the automaton is how it further multiplies the duality into a triad of selves.

> [N]ot a soul without a body, but [...] a body without a soul! [...] For an instant he seemed to see this unnatural contest between a *dead intelligence* and a *breathing mechanism* only as a *spectator*—such fancies are in dreams; then here gained his *identity* almost as if by a leap forward into his body, and the straining *automaton* had a directing will as alert and fierce as that of its hideous antagonist." [emphasis added] (7-8)

The split inherent in the dualities of "a body without a soul," "a breathing mechanism," and those of its mirroring phrases in "a soul without a body," "dead intelligence" is a "leap forward" the outer, third self, that of the "spectator". Yet, this explosion is also an implosion at the same time. The conflicting drama of a compulsive return to the trauma is played out to the effect of reaching its climax by ejecting the singularity of identity and rendering it a "spectator" of its own dissemination. At this point, "Halpin Frayser dreamed that he was dead" (8). The infinite, spiraling cycle of compulsions to repeat is corroborated by loops: "the combat's result is the combat's cause" (8). Halpin Frayser's dreamed death signals the collapse of the narrative. Paradoxically, this break down is also a *denouement* reaching a mechanical sense of the sublime not unparalleled by Lovecraft's automata and "daemons of unplumbed space" (*Supernatural* 15). "The Death of Halpin Frayser" concludes with the plurality of disseminating voices ever distancing themselves from and vanishing in the infinite singularity of sublime silence. "As it had grown out of *silence*, so now it died away; from a *culminating* shout which had seemed almost in their ears, it drew itself away into the distance, until its failing notes, joyless and *mechanical* to the last, sank to silence at a *measureless remove*" [emphasis added] (15).

What makes Henry James's "Sir Edmund Orme" (1891) yet another labyrinthine example for the triads inherent in the automaton is the delicate dance around numerous permutations of threes that number five offers in the characters of (1) the narrator, (2) Sir Edmund Orme, (3) Mrs. Marden, (4) Charlotte Marden, and (5) Captain Marden. Sir Edmund Orme is transformed into a pale, vague, strange, cold and silent automaton at the instance his love chose Captain Marden over him, yet he was never present again until his rival's death. It is only when there appear only three characters out of the possible five on stage that this drama of retribution can move towards a new phase in the sequence of events. Previous to the narrator's encounter with the Mardens, the triad consisted of the singularity of the spectral automaton (as compulsive return to the trauma of his death), the mother and her *Doppelgänger*, Charlotte Marden (as the innocent, would-be substitute sacrifice). The first outsider to whom the "perfect presence" (865, 866) of Sir Edmund Orme appears is the narrator, who becomes an accomplice to the mother. Mrs. Marden willingly gives advantage to the young gentleman over other suitors in exchange for finally sharing a most foreboding secret with an outsider: "'You *have* intervened,' she sobbed; 'You're *in* it, you're *in* it" [emphasis in original] (866). The two men become doubles when the soundless apparition of the ghost is put in parallel with the silence of the narrator: "I held my tongue for three months" (875). Now it is the ghost's turn to disappear from the triad of the Mardens and the Narrator, who acknowledges with relief that "Sir Edmund Orme gave us a holiday" (875). It seems that the absence of his *Doppelgänger* instigates the narrator's detachment from Charlotte: "I felt less connected, less designated with Charlotte" (Ibid.). But, when the mother falls ill, happiness is made possible for Charlotte and the narrator by the deadly duality of the ghost of Sir Edmund Orme and the sinful Mrs. Marden. Through the impossibility of "not knowing which was which" (878), the romantic couple is turned into a pair of mirror images. This duality is complemented into a triad by the trauma of the reciprocal murders. "The transcendent essence" (873) as a mirroring third element makes them one in a similar vein the reciprocal murders of the Larues created their singleness. Charlotte is saved from becoming a substitute sacrifice by the ghastly and ghostly union between her mother and Sir Edmund Orme, who from "perfect presence" (865, 866) is thus reduced to an "unmentionable presence" for the subsequent generations: a story never to be told (874).

I held her there a moment – bending over her, given up to her, feeling each of her throbs with my own and not knowing which was which; then, all of a sudden, coldly, I gathered that we were alone. She released herself. The figure beside the sofa had vanished; but Mrs Marden lay in her place with closed eyes, with something in her stillness that gave us both another terror. Charlotte expressed it in the cry of "Mother, mother!" with which she flung herself down. I fell on my knees beside her. Mrs Marden had passed away. [...] [T]hat was, mercifully, the last of Sir Edmund Orme. (878)

Meme in genre transmutation

The *Alien* franchise created by Ridley Scott, just as the already mentioned first piece of John Carpenter's *Apocalypse Trilogy*: *The Thing* (1982) is widely celebrated as the most compelling transmutations of Lovecraftian memes. As Roger Luckhurst insists: "After Giger had cross-pollinated the Alien franchise with Lovecraft, the series has repeatedly returned to Lovecraft as an inspiration (*Prometheus* most of all)" (58). In his short piece, "The Whisperer in Darkness" (1930) the singularity of the story not to be told presents itself as the utter dread of the unknown. "Cosmic horror" (709) is the prime mover in the *Alien* series as well—the back story of which remains arcane after the sixth core film has been released. The split of number two between body and soul (Bierce 7) in Lovecraft's narrative is indexed first by a rasping phonograph record and insectile buzzes both mechanizing human voice, then the "the face and hands of Henry Wentworth Akeley" (*The Fiction* 722) as fragmented components of robotized corporeality, and ultimately, the removed "bodiless and mechanical" (710) brain in the shiny cylinder evocative of the soul's detachment from the unity of "identity" (722). There is a radical shift, however, in the employment of the automaton meme from what could be observed in he previously analyzed short stories by Bierce and James. Here, the compulsive return to the unspeakable horror is allegorized in a concept of the automaton which becomes combined with such biological monstrosities as "cormophytic fungi" (696) and "toad-like" creatures (708). Also, whereas the implosion and collapse of triads in the previously interpreted two stories offered an end-driven narrative structure, Lovecraft's poetics opens his stories up to endless sequels, variations, multiplications by empowering the automaton to mutate by contamination in "The Dunwich Horror" and serialization in "Herbert West—Reanimator". "To be brief and plain, the machine with the tubes and sound-box began to speak [...]. I expect to have the pleasure of Mr. Akeley's company. I wish I might have yours as well" (712). Automata fused with organisms that have the capacity to copy themselves present two innovations or rather mutations in the Lovecraftian universe that remerge in both Carpenter's trilogy and Scott's franchise. As Luckhurst observes:

In each core *Alien* film, the alien is always coupled with the robot or
symbiont as the other vector of threat to human integrity. This is a properly
cybernetic understanding that humans must now be placed in an array of
systems and environments, that the ecology of our lives extends beyond the
biosphere and now includes technological ensembles like the *Nostromo*, its
interstellar networks and its autonomous machines. [...] [T]he symmetry of
machine and beast is emphasised [...]. (68)

This emphasis is expressed by coupling robotic characters (Ash, Bishop) with
a proliferation of beasts. The plethora of aliens include such diverse array of
monsters as the Queen, xenomorphs, drones, facehuggers, chestbursters,
dragons, newborns, predaliens, neomorphs, protomorphs: an engineered
biological taxonomy that finds its source and inspiration in an eldritch
pantheon of abominable creatures with the likes of Cthulhu, Azathoth,
Nyarlathotep, Tsathoggua, Yog-Sothoth, Hastur, Dagon, Shub-Niggurath...

iv. Chance and Uncanny Coincidences

Freud affirms that the act of repetition is what presents itself as the decisive
factor in the uncanny nature of chance events and coincidences when he
states:

> [W]e have no difficulty in recognizing that it is only the factor of unintended
> repetition that transforms what would otherwise seem quite harmless into
> something uncanny and forces us to entertain the idea of the fateful and the
> inescapable, when we should normally speak of "chance." (144)

Return as a compulsive impulse to indicate the absence of a presupposed
unity also incorporates another allegorization within itself, that of
Doppelgängers. The rhyming pair of coincidences created in the act of
perception is a propelling force of signification that exhibits parallels with
what has already been outlined in the discussion of doubles. Whenever
uncanny coincidences occur in a narrative, it is the sublime of an ever absent,
yet inamissible singularity that is being defined as the aesthetic stake in telling
the story. Yet, there is a significant shift detectable between *Doppelgängers* and
coincidences from subjectivation towards meaning creation. "Unintended
repetition" (Ibid.) can only be interpreted as repetition initially unmarked for
intention, since the return is always-already between disparate, random
elements, which are intentionalized into meaningful, coherent, rhyming pairs
"of the fateful and the inescapable" (Ibid.). The paradox lies in the fact that
the very act of assigning meaning to coupled occurrences already renders
meaning preexistent, in consequence, repetition can never be unintended. As

Jean-François Lyotard insists: "In the case of the subject, and by consequence the other as subject (that is, as *alter ego*), we cannot *reduce* the real existence to an intentional correlate, since what I intentionalize when I see the other is precisely an absolute existence: here, being real and being intentional merge together" [emphasis in original] (58). Interpreting the presence of two elements as duplicated, coincidentally reemerging phenomena of a singularity always conveys a turn (trope) from sequence of events to diverse plots, from incongruous, haphazard sememes to possible meanings, from isolated movements to compulsive returns towards a locus never to be reached.

The aporia between intentionalized and unintended meanings in chance events as a tension and impetus for uncanny narratives is central to William Fryer Harvey's short fiction "August Heat" written in 1910. Harvey's story finds its memetic counterpart, for instance, in Stephen King's "The Dune" (2011). In the note that accompanies each of the short stories in the *Bazaar of Bad Dreams*, King recounts a chance event that made his story "arrive" (81) seemingly out of thin air. The author describes the genesis of "The Dune" as an uncanny coincidence between a real life chance event of sunlight and shadow tricking him to see writing in the sand where there was nothing. An undecidability and uncertainty in the Todorovian sense lie between the rhyming pairs, in the act of mistaking something for something else. At the end of his note, Stephen King compares his story revolving around coincidences with Harvey's classic.

The narration of "August Heat" is built exclusively on a rigorous economy of words, and efficient mastery of plot development for the single reason that there is no denouement. Everything that is described, recounted in the discourse is retrospectively governed by this narrative fissure, which, for lack of a proper resolution, dislocates the space of meaning production to a territory of utter uncertainty. The concluding lines: "It is enough to send a man mad" (238) refers the reader back to the rhyming games of signifiers played out on the previous four pages by asserting the irrationality of the climax. Madness—which will be expounded on as another allegorization of the uncanny in the ensuing section— thus, constrains narrative tension within opposing and mutually exclusive limits. Perception becomes a constant hesitation between what is unintended and what is intentional. No matter what the foreboding last concluding lines suggest, none of the *Doppelgängers* go insane by the end of the story, here incoherence and absurdity are but a *caveat*. Yet, signification is directed back to a ghost-like state, to what Derrida called in *Specters of Marx* "hauntology." This concept connects the always-already absent present with an understanding of language that is dependent on a system of linguistic differences prior to its origin. Derrida contends that "the radical possibility of all spectrality should be sought in the direction that Husserl identifies, in such surprising but forceful way, as an intentional but *non-real* [*non-réelle*] component of the phenomenological lived experience [...]" (237).

The house of the monumental mason, who is a *Doppelgänger* for the narrator is a haunted place: "I don't know about oasis but it certainly is hot, hot as hell" (235). This spectral quality is fused with irrationality, here the stifling heat is "enough to send a man mad" (238), but a fourth allegorization also merges with the presence of chance events. The two characters operate like puppets, *automata* as references without referents, embodiments of Lyotard's transcendent object (54). The protagonist rolls up his sketch and "without knowing why" places it in his pocket (Harvey 235). A "sudden impulse" makes him enter the mason's workshop (Ibid.). The mason puts down the "first name that came" into his head (236). Finally the artist/protagonist meets his demise by declaring that "To my surprise I agreed" (237). "It's a rum go" (Ibid.) indeed as the mason acknowledges, it must be but an "unnatural, uncanny" and "strange coincidence" that an artist should put down the execution scene of his future murderer the same morning when the yet innocent mason inscribes his would-be victim's name on a tombstone (236). The linear narration of the draughtsman, who creates two dimensional drawings, ushers the reader to his *Doppelgänger,* the mason carving letters in a three dimensional piece of stone. They both function as *automata* operated by mere coincidences and the madness that looms over the haunted house, which is characterized with phrases, such as "curiously veined marble" (235), "headstones" (236), "the air seems charged with thunder," "shaky table," "the leg is cracked" (238). Anything could happen, possibly real meanings multiply around the lack of semantic abyss: "A cart may run you over, and there's always banana skins and orange peel, to say nothing of falling ladders" (237). Yet, there is one thing that the story circumspectly and painstakingly avoids telling. The collapse of coinciding doubles into one, single preexisting entity through the act of an unreal, inexplicable murder.

In Lovecraft's "The Shadow Out of Time" (1936) two different time dimensions provide a continuous flux of synchronicity for rhyming coincidences. "My conception of time, my ability to distinguish between consecutiveness and simultaneousness seemed subtly disordered" (954), concedes the protagonist. In parallel with W. F. Harvey's short story, Lovecraft's conception of chance events, madness as the irrationality of signification, and *automata* are ever-present: "I believed I was indeed going mad" (956). Simultaneity and irrationality is accentuated in the blurred intersection of conscious and semi-conscious states: "I was awake and dreaming at the same time," haunted by "maddening dreams" (982). Just as in the case his predecessor's narrative, Lovecraft's piece amalgamates madness with the impending doom of turning animate beings into *automata*: "Alien captive minds inhabiting their bodies" (971). The crucial difference in the way the two authors utilize tropes of the uncanny is that Lovecraft, who is overtly preoccupied with creating an atmosphere of cosmic horror, embeds these allegorizations in *mise-en-abymes*. The cone shaped bodies of the Yithians are the mortal coil of a race previously annihilated by a mass projection of minds (a myth leading back to the Elder Things), and it is also revealed that the Great Race of Yith will possess new bodies after humanity has disappeared from the face of the Earth. The *mise-en-abymic* structure underpinned by three possible allegorizations of the uncanny is also central to the conclusion of the story. Here, the "blasphemous reachings and seizures in the cosmos-wide vortex of time" aligns with the protagonist's realization that, in the "abyss" of the archive, the "eon browned" pages containing an unspeakable secret of the unplumbed cosmos are written in his own handwriting (998). The content of the book-within-the-book remains unknown and untold.

Coincidences are among the most significant narrative devices that endow Lovecraft's plot with the atmosphere of cosmic horror. "The Temple" written in 1920 is typical in this respect by its juxtaposition of two artefacts. "*The head of the radiant god in the sculptures on the rock temple is the same as that carven bit of ivory which the dead sailor brought from the sea and which poor Klenze carried back into the sea.* I was a little dazed by this coincidence" [emphasis in original] (99). The narrative function that this chance event carries out seems purely technical at first glance, it purportedly thrusts plot development toward creating a mystery, which, in turn, generates a need for resolution. Yet, no resolution, no disclosure of enigma is offered in the story. After an accident renders the submarine immobile, upon finding the temple, Klenze, the Lieutenant of the U-boat, succumbs to insane paranoia and finally dies. Altberg, who previously ordered the remaining crew of the U.S. warship to be executed, mesmerized by the sublime flickering light of the underwater altar willingly meets his own death. It is never explained whether the mysterious temple—which is only suggested to be the source of auditory hallucinations—is surrounded by the ruined city of Atlantis, or R'lyeh, nor is the content of the sealed manuscript ever revealed in the story. The undecidabilities and chance events in the narrative lead any act of signification back to two opposing realities, which cancel each other out. The head of the radiant god is both an archeological find and an harbinger of death, just as the temple is the remnant of Atlantis and R'lyeh at the same time. The mythic cycle is left incomplete for the sake of the same aesthetic effect that prevented Lovecraft from publishing the Necronomicon or the myth of Cthulhu as unified, coherent narratives. For it is in the utter hesitation and sustained uncertainty where an atmosphere of ultimate dread from the cosmic horror of the unknown becomes experienced.

Meme in genre transmutation

The chamber drama of *The Mist* (2007) as one of the most highly acclaimed movie inspired by the Lovecraftian *oeuvre* is revolving around coincidences, accidents as well. The film is about a group of ordinary people, who, by incident, happen to be at the location where Project Arrowhead, a government experiment to open a gateway to other dimensions, goes terribly wrong. Lovecraftian creatures overrun the once sleepy town, yet the plot focuses on the different ways denizens interpret, make sense of the chance event that cast them between the opposite ends of real and unreal, between the coinciding pairs of a randomized rhyme. Again, what seems at stake initially is meaning making: whether it is a bigoted Mrs. Carmody praying for salvation from what she sees as Armageddon or the practical-minded Norton, or rather the nameless woman fearing for her children who will be successful in surviving. But ascribing meaning to a chance event is utterly futile in this possible world since its territory of dislocation is that of utter uncertainty, an area covered in mist. Neither the reality, nor the irrationality of the situation offers a climax or resolution for the plot of the movie: Project Arrowhead is concluded by closing down the portal to another dimension that still remains a constant threat. In their stead, reiterating all efforts of meaning creation, the accident of missing a coincidence in the conclusion defines chance event as the prime motivation in the narration. Although she seemed only a digressive element at the outset to signal the foreboding future, the unnamed woman, who first left the store with her children and was supposed to be the first victim, reappears in the final scene alive and intact. In the closure, the enduring protagonist, David kills all the other survivors to save them from an inevitably horrifying end only to realize seconds later that the army has overcome the monstrous invaders. His final scream marks the impossibility of searching for a singular signified connecting the rhyming binaries in chance events.

v. Madness and Atemporality

> The uncanny effect of epilepsy or madness has the same origin. Here the layman sees a manifestation of forces that he did not suspect in a fellow human being, but whose stirrings he can dimly perceive in remote corners of his own personality. [...] Let us add something of a general nature, which is, strictly speaking, already contained in what we have previously said about animism and the superannuated workings of our mental apparatus, but seems to call for special emphasis. This is the fact that an uncanny effect often arises when the boundary between fantasy and reality is blurred, when we are faced with the reality of something that we have until now considered

imaginary, when a symbol takes on the full function and significance of what it symbolizes, and so forth. This is at the root of much that is uncanny about magical practices. (Freud 150-151)

From the perspective of the present exploration two observations of the above excerpt has to be highlighted. First, when discussing madness, Freud's argument inadvertently places the ego in relation to the other turning them into *Doppelgängers*, thus localizing madness in the utter hesitation between the self and its mirroring other. An abysmal conformation of madness as utter uncertainty between interior and exterior is what Michel Foucault's *Madness and Civilization* conceptualizes: "Madness has become man's possibility of abolishing both man and the world [...] because it is the ambiguity of chaos and apocalypse" (281). Repetition, reciprocal oscillation between a preexistent, presupposed origin and irrational signifying processes are postulates in Foucault's work (286). Secondly, in the above excerpt by Freud the blurred boundary between reality and fantasy in animism and uncanny magical practices is put them in an equation with a unity of symbol and symbolized. These primordial modes of signification subvert temporality in the sense that the "full function and significance" (Freud 151) in the irrationality of the monadic symbol is inherently atemporal. For this latter attribute the "Red Room" in David Lynch's *Twin Peaks* offers itself as a conspicuous illustration. John A. Michon delineating J. T. Fraser's levels of temporality identifies mysticism and animism as root metaphors for atemporality (60). Fraser himself connects the notion of atemporality with the chaos of the underworld when asserting that

> [a]temporality is not to be mistaken for the philosophical idea of nothingness. It might better be associated with the pre-Socratic notion of Chaos, a state of affairs which was said to have preceded the emergence of the world. [...] Some of the early Greek cosmogonists identified Chaos with Tartaros, a sunless abyss and the lowest part of the underworld. (*The Genesis and Evolution of Time* 31)

The vertiginous atemporality of madness as a meme for the "full function and significance" of typological symbols, prefigurations as chance coincidences refer to one single but inaccessible meaning (Freud 151). Thus, timelessness in derangement creates one another trope of the uncanny that connects Lovecraft's *oeuvre* with his highly canonized predecessors. The lines already cited from "The Dreams in the Witch House" (1932) with regard to the *mise-en-abymical* structure of spaces in the Lovecraftian universe could well be interpreted as a direct allusion to Charlotte Perkins Gilman's "The Yellow Wall-Paper" (1892): "Gilman's room was of good size but queerly irregular shape; [...] there was no access—nor any appearance of a former avenue of access—to the space which must have existed between the slanting wall and the straight outer wall on the house's north side [...]" (861).

A space containing larger expanse than itself is described in Gilman's short story as a "queer" and "haunted house" (166). The sub-pattern (171, 176) behind the wallpaper that opens up the mirroring plane of the "woman" (174, 176, 178) to the irrational perception of the protagonist has no access for "reason" personified in the husband (169), who would find even the existence of it "absurd" (173). Irrationality is indexed by the recurring sign of the Moon (167, 174, 176, 180), while the atemporal synchronicity of signification is first indicated by the mentioning of "arbors" (167, 179, 170) and "garden" (167, 169, 172, 179), both of which serve as prefigurations for a yet undisclosed, *unheimlich* space. The distinction between prefiguration and fulfillment breaks down when the woman's ghostly creeping is brought to daylight.

> I see her in that long shaded lane, creeping up and down. I see her in those dark grape arbors, creeping all around the garden. I see her on that long road under the trees, creeping along, and when a carriage comes she hides under the blackberry vines. I don't blame her a bit. It must be very humiliating to be caught creeping by daylight! (179)

In the multiple descriptions of the patterns in the wallpaper verbs expressing motion are used to mirror the eye-movement of the perceiver. The only dynamic verb that is an exception is "commit suicide" (168). Copulas, verbs with stative meaning such as "match" (160), "stare" (170), "connect" (172) are prevalent in these ekphrases. Patterns create an atemporal space of "everlastingness" (170) with their rhizome-like qualities: "an interminable string of toadstools, budding and sprouting in endless convolution" (175). On the other hand, a proliferation of indices marks the recurrent returns to the inaccessible singularity of meaning: "nobody could climb through that pattern—it strangles so; I think that is why it has so many heads" (178). The story of the woman behind the bars wrought by the patterns is never to be read by the ratiocinative husband, whose fainting signifies the collapse of all boundaries between the rational and the irrational. Memetic attributes such as the adjective "bulbous" will reappear, for instance, in Lovecraft's "At the Mountains of Madness" (738, 746, 762), along with the synesthetic smell as an index hinting at, implying the presence of the uncanny (741, 786, 801). Textual occurrences, such as "pointless pattern," "not arranged on any laws," "I exhaust myself in trying to distinguish the order," "confusion" (172) are not only expressive of madness in "The Yellow Wall-Paper" but also of the atemporality in a dreamlike state that is characteristic of the weird: "optic horror" in "delirium tremens" (Ibid.). At the climax of Gilman's narrative, the lifeless yet animate automaton of the husband's body is presented as an allegorization for the story not to be told, the inaccessible trauma "over" and to—but not *in*—which the creeping, weird protagonist compulsively returns "every time" (182).

Ambrose Bierce's "An Occurrence at Owl Creek Bridge" (1890) also fuses atemporality and irrationality in a dreamlike state. Its handling of time is the single most distinctive narrative device in the entirety of the text offering itself as a governing trope for a story that focuses on frozen time. The first three paragraphs of the introductory section is a still life of the execution scene, a meticulous ekphrasis composed completely of descriptive statements, whereas the ensuing three paragraphs narrates a sequence of actions with ever decreasing pace. This symmetry of proportion is indicative of a tripartite structure from static stance through actions recounted with a gradual slowing-down of the tempo back to atemporality in the final paragraph. The second phase weaves the concept of time slowing down with (1) madness, (2) the *mise-en-abymic* symbol of vortex, and (3) water as a symbol for dreams. "He looked a moment at his 'unsteadfast footing,' then let his gaze wander to the swirling water of the stream racing madly beneath his feet. A piece of dancing driftwood caught his attention and his eyes followed it down the current. How slowly it appeared to move! What a sluggish stream"! Here, in two sentences the pace decelerates from "racing madly" to "sluggish" (24). With an inversion, the succeeding paragraph associates the notion of madness now with prolonged intervals further decreasing the already sluggardly tempo. The penultimate paragraph merges the symbol of water with a picture of the family to be left behind and introduces the symbol of a device measuring time. "The intervals of silence grew progressively longer; the delays became maddening. [...] What he heard was the ticking of his watch" (25). Interrupted by soundless pauses, finally the progressive slowing down is brought to a halt, to an atemporality of signification in the concluding paragraph: "these thoughts [...] were flashed into the doomed man's brain rather than evolved from it" (26).

The second section gives a short recount in chronological order relating the antecedents that lead to the execution of Peyton Farquhar. The third one by inserting phrases, such as "as one already dead," "without material substance," "he had power only to feel," however, emphasizes the atemporality of the discourse right at the outset by describing a peternaturally rapid pulsation of time, which turns pure perception into the uncanny symbol of an unthinkable sense of time: "unthinkable arcs of oscillation," "like a vast pendulum" (29).

Corporeality and emotions being separated, a "feeling of fullness" (29) comes over the protagonist, who perceives an animistic world in the totality of synchronicity: "He was now in full possession of his physical senses. They were, indeed, peternaturally keen and alert" (31). "Vortex" and "gyration" (36) are indices for an atemporal, *pars pro toto* space that opens up to vistas of a dreamlike territory of timeless originary nature: "aeolian harps," "[t]he forest seemed interminable," "[t]here was something uncanny in the revelation" (36-37). The last section sets out with the symbol of bodiless atemporality and concludes in the return to temporality with the image Peyton Farquhar's corpse swinging like a pendulum: "Peyton Farquhar was dead; his body, with a broken neck, swung gently from side to side beneath the timbers of the Owl Creek bridge" (39). The narrative frame encapsulates the traumatic lack of a story that cannot be told for the reason that it never took place in the first place. Where it did occur, however, is nowhere else but the atemporal, irrational, uncanny location of the transient "Owl Creek Bridge."

In "The Shadow Out of Time" analyzed in the previous section it is a coalescence of dream (repeated in its various forms 113 times on 51 pages), madness (the stem and its synonyms appear 26 times), and time (as a noun used 29 times) that creates the domain of atemporal and irrational signification. In Lovecraft's novella "At the Mountains of Madness" the very same allegorization of the uncanny is found in elaborate descriptions of rock formations and eldritch, otherwordly architecture. These descriptions play a decisive role in Lovecraftian poetics as discussed to in detail by Houellebecq, who devotes an entire chapter of "Then You Will See a Magnificent Cathedral" to them. in his book on the author. Quoting Lovecraft's correspondence with Kleiner, the French writer underlines the atemporal, irrational qualities of these textual loci: "And it was in all seriousness he told Kleiner that a man is like a coral insect—that his only destiny is to '*build vast beautiful, mineral things for the moon to delight in after he is dead*'" [emphasis in original] (65). An art form in itself conveying a sense of atemporal readings of space, architecture is defined in the Lovecraftian *oeuvre* with a prefix giving negative force, as non-Euclidian, which term—as previously discussed—emphasizes the uncanny characteristics of these structures. The language Lovecraft created to depict eldritch monuments, buildings, rock formations is seen as his highest, most revered stylistic achievement on a par with classics by his Romantic predecessors, and often characterized as a plethora of paroxisms by Houellebecq (71, 82). This effect is brought about by the impossible effort to name the unnamable, to grasp the sublime atemorality of radical dislocation. In "At the Mountains of Madness," Lovecraft centers depictions of Cyclopean constructions on such tropes as the *mise-en-abymic* vortex, the paradox of the ultimate name that cannot be uttered, also, atemporaility and madness. The principles that govern the designs of "the unnamable architecture of time" (79) are built on a juxtaposition of incompatible, inconsistent, and irreconcilable dimensions and spectra. Houellebecq distilled the aesthetics of H. P. Lovecraft in barely six words: "The scale factor, the vertigo factor" (81).

Several places in the novella exhibit traits of the typological symbolism and synchronicity in the magical mode of signification discussed at the beginning of this section. Lovecraft explains that the uncanny structures "had been shaped to greater symmetry by some magic hand" (755), just as instances for prefigurations and their fulfillment are offered in the text. The makeshift dwellings of the explorers are mirrored in the campsite they chance upon. "In other words, it could not be other than a sort of camp—a camp made by questing beings who like us had been turned back by the unexpectedly choked way to the abyss" (787). Meaning creation as an irrational effort to access the presupposed singularity in the blurred domain between the real and the imaginary is described here as a compulsive drive for repetition: "weaving links betwixt this lost world and some of my own wildest dreams concerning the mad horror at the camp" (759).

As a counterpart for the homeliness of the camp, the *unheimlich* "magnificent cathedral" (Houellebecq 63) erected by the Old Ones is also doubled in atemporal signification. The sacred nature of Lovecraftian architecture is epitomized in theological prefigurations that are suggestive of sublime horror in unearthly dimensions (66).

> [T]his shocking stone survival had projected its image across the mountains according to the simple laws of reflection. Of course the phantom had been twisted and exaggerated, and had contained things which the real source did not contain; yet now, as we saw that real source, we thought it even more hideous and menacing than its distant image. (757)

It is not just the previously quoted ever-present smell of decay that makes Lovecraft's descriptions reminiscent of Charlotte Perkins Gilman's short story. Citing a typical illustration for the Lovecraftian paroxism in depicting otherwordly architecture brings back not only the vocabulary, but also the irrationality inherent in the representation of patterns in the yellow wallpaper: "There were geometrical forms for which an Euclid could scarcely find a name—cones of all degrees of irregularity and truncation; terraces of every sort of *provocative* disproportion; shafts with odd *bulbous* enlargements; *broken* columns in curious groups; and five-pointed or five-ridged arrangements of mad *grotesqueness*" [emphasis added] (762).

The countless instances of the words "madness"(nineteen times), "mirages" (twelve times on eighty-three pages), and juxtaposed disproportionate time scales are deployed in the novella to create a vertiginous atmosphere directed towards the unspeakable and unnamable. "The bottomless abyss" (763) of "illimitable emptiness" (764) guides the reader to the singularity that cannot be accessed. As Houellebecq contends: "'All-in-One and One-in-All'. [...] These are the coordinates of the unnamable" (82-83). Lovecraft concludes his story with an intensely poignant sense of humor. Having reemerged from the bottomless depths of the abyss, an insane Danforth keeps repeating the unnamable he risked his life for, but all that is heard is the absurdly eldritch cry of the penguins: "Tekeli-li! Tekeli-li!" (806).

Meme in genre transmutation

John Carpenter's final installation of *Apocalypse Trilogy* entitled *In the Mouth of Madness* (an intended pun on and reference to Lovecraft's novella) swirls around madness and atemporality in *mise-en-abymic*, metaleptic abysses. With regard to memes taken from Lovecraft, "The Shadow Out of Time" can be identified as a main source of inspiration for time shifts and automaton characters, however, both these features are reiterated with a postmodern twist. The plot is propelled forward by the mystery, which is buried in an ominous book entitled *In the Mouth of Madness* and written by a certain Stutter Cane. Cane's book is set in Hobb's End, which serves as the atemporal, vertiginous center for a series of metaleptic teleportations in the movie. A time distortion transports the protagonist John Trent and his charming companion, Linda Styles to the exact replica of the town, a spatial echo, as it were. Upon confronting Cane, Linda is driven mad by the book, the story of which is never to be told in the film. Trent tries to escape, but his return to the center of the town is made compulsive and inevitable by yet another teleportation. Now it is the protagonist's turn to face the fictitious writer, who reveals that Trent is a character in his book. Trent now has a doubled identity as an insurance investigator— an index for a tragic Oedipal hero— and an imaginary deathmonger. In this latter role, Trent is forced to play his scripted part and return the manuscript to the publisher, so its mysterious story can contaminate and annihilate humanity. At this point the fictitious writer turns himself into a portal by way of tearing his face open. After being chased by Lovecraftian monsters in the tunnel of the portal, the protagonist is teleported back to reality with a time shift. The manuscript has already been delivered months before, even a movie adaptation is to be released as memetic transmutation in genre formations. In the final scene the protagonist is watching the movie the audience has been watching all along including a scene where Trent is shouting the words: "This is reality." The joke is on Trent, the audience, and mankind. Trent bursts into a hysterical laugh then breaks down in tears.

No matter how different this plot may seem from what the reader finds "At the Mountains of Madness," the meme of the sour and poignant humor is exactly the same in both tales of the weird.

vi. Humor

Freud merely touches upon the subject matter of humor in his 1919 essay, yet the significance of humor as one of the six tropes of the uncanny has an undeniably manifest impact both on Freudian psychoanalysis and past and contemporary genre formations.

> The factor of the repetition of the same thing will perhaps not be acknowledged by everyone as a source of the sense of the uncanny. According to my own observations it undoubtedly evokes such a feeling under particular conditions, and in combination with particular circumstances – a feeling, moreover, that recalls the helplessness we experience in certain dream-states. [...] One may, for instance, have lost one's way in the woods, perhaps after being overtaken by fog, and, despite all one's efforts to find a marked or familiar path, one comes back again and again to the same spot, which one recognizes by a particular physical feature. Or one may be groping around in the dark in an unfamiliar room, searching for the door or the light-switch and repeatedly colliding with the same piece of furniture – a situation that Mark Twain has transformed, admittedly by means of grotesque exaggeration, into something irresistibly comic. (143-144)

Out of the many photographs that were taken of H. P. Lovecraft there are three images that stand out in particular, all of which were shot on the same day: the 5th of July in 1921. One shows the author with his beloved wife and true companion, Sonia Greene, the other with his friend, William J. Dowdell, and a third in the company of George Julian Houtain. These pictures are virally famous for the simple reason that there are no other photos on which Lovecraft can be seen smiling. It must have been a beautiful day radiating love, comradery and friendship. Just as Dowdell, Houtain too was an amateur journalist, the founder of *Home Brew,* a humor magazine for which Lovecraft wrote "Herbert West—Reanimator" between 1921 and 1922. As is indicated by analyses in the previous section on madness, the unique humor in Lovecraftian narratives and its memetic mutations inspired by the American author has to be differentiated from a propensity towards slapstick comedy that characterizes, for instance, the crossover genre of horredy, which will be discussed in detail later. Lovecraft's serene portrayals are emblematic of one essential quality in his poetics. His listless facial expression is a meme in itself echoing not only the title of Houellebecq's monograph on Lovecraftian amorality: *Against the World, Against Life,* but also Foucault's observation in *Madness and Civilization*: "The nothingness of unreason, in which the language of Nature had died forever, has become a violence of Nature and against Nature, to the point of the savage abolition of itself" (285). The hardships H. P. Lovecraft endured throughout his life and in his literary career, just as the overwhelming memetic influence his *oeuvre* keep exerting on present and future generations yet to come are generally attributed to a radical and subversive emptying out of reassuring beliefs in binary systems, such as human vs. nature, individual vs. god, the familiarity of the interior vs. the unknown exterior. The introduction written to the complete and unabridged collection of his works summarizes a general consensus: "Most interesting of all, Lovecraft himself has become a cultural icon, his gaunt, lantern-jawed countenance immediately recognizable as the fitting visage of one whose imagination populated the world with a legion of cosmic horrors that bleakly underscored the insignificance of humanity and all its works in a blind, godless universe" (Lovecraft *The Fiction* ix). When looking for humor in the Lovecraftian universe, it is mad guffaws, the absurd, chaotic implosion of the self that is exhibited in, for instance, the concluding "Tekeli-li" (806) of "At the Mountains of Madness," or in the final paragraphs of "The Call of Cthulhu": "Briden looked back and went mad, laughing shrilly as he kept on laughing at intervals till death found him one night in the cabin whilst Johansen was wandering deliriously" (378).

The sixth allegorization of the uncanny had a foreboding significance for Lovecraft, whose humor cannot be described in terms of such traditional approaches as the superiority theory, that is, laughing at something with a sense of being above, or the relief theory, which negotiates laughter resulting in release of tension. The incongruity theory occupies a different perspective by locating the source of laughter in an uncanny experience that violates expectations projected by previously constructed cognitive patterns, thus generating an inaccessible inconsistency (Morreall 245). According to this theory, a tension mounted between irreconcilable realities is what is resolved by laughing—any sketch by Monty Python could be used here as a textbook example. Michael Clark in *The Philosophy of Laughter and Humor* defines three criteria that are necessary to create such an effect. A person (1) perceives something as incongruous, (2) *enjoys* perceiving it as such, and finally (3) does so for the sake of incongruity itself and not for physiological release, or with the intention of feeling superior (139-155). But, when probing into the capacity of incongruity, Mike W. Martin offers examples when amusement resulting in laugh is not the only way for the audience to enjoy incongruity. The illustration he gives is Sophocles' *Oedipus the King*, where the incongruity of the king's vow to do everything in his power to find King Laius' murderer creates a tension in the audience, who are well aware of Oedipus' patricide. The aesthetic effect is not that of humor, yet it still causes aesthetic pleasure. The intriguing, uncanny aspect in the essays edited by John Morreall, *The Philosophy of Laughter and Humor* is that they lead step by step from accounts for laughter towards explications of amazement and confusion. In the final third of the book Morreall takes Martin's concept a step further by confirming that such aesthetic categories as the horrible, the fantastic, the macabre, and the grotesque, though built exclusively on uncanny incongruities, entail a non-humorous amusement in transgressions against horizons of expectations. As he contends: "What we enjoy here is being surprised by strange things and situations" (205). As can be observed in the evolution of theories of humor, the weird tale swirling around uncanny inconsistencies always-already involves the element of humor, just as humor has always had the capacity to incorporate the uncanny as the basis of tensions to be resolved in laughter. Lovecraft's aesthetic invention is to push limitless incongruities to the extreme, to create situations where humor collides with sheer madness and callous indifference in absolute amorality—as illustrated by the paragraph cited in the motto above. The frequently quoted line he wrote in defense of "Dagon" is the sole exception when he commented: "But I cannot help seeing beyond the tinsel of humour, and recognizing the pitiful basis of jest—the world is indeed comic, but the joke is on mankind" (Lovecraft *[In Defense]* 54).

The aesthetic potential for humor is always-already memetic as an aesthetic quality derived from incongruities that the genre of uncanny tales encapsulates. Parallel with the emergence of early gothic tales in American literature influenced by the works of Horace Walpole and Ann Radcliffe, there appeared the first comic reiterations. "The Lightning-Rod Man" (1856) by Herman Melville is a play on genre expectations and incongruities to comical effect. Stylistically the short story is embellished by a vast array of hyperboles ranging from overly stylized exclamations—"Hark!" repeated ten times on six pages—through ancient Latin vocabulary and mythological images: hills are "acroceraunian" (118), a chair is a substitute for the "evergreen throne on Olympus"(119). Finally, this stylistic extravaganza is pushed to downright exaggerations: the cottage can be turned into "Gibraltar", roars of thunder are described as "Himalayas of concussions" (120). The dealer in lightning-rods, a door-to-door salesman in actuality is addressed as "Jupiter Tonans" or "Thundering Jupiter" (119, 120, 124), "Tetzel," who was the *casus belli* for Protestantism, "false negotiator" or the "dark lightning-king" (124). The host when scolded, chided and blamed for his unpardonable nescience is deemed a "horridly ignorant" (119) and "impious wretch" (124). The stake of the debate is whether the dealer will manage to sell his copper lightning-rod for a dollar a foot—a reference to Benjamin Franklin, the enlightened scientist and his thirteen virtues— or if the host devoted to a benevolent Deity will finally manage to kick the sales hustler out of his home without having spent a dime. The entire setting is not only a parody of the memetic opening sentence for gothic stories: "It was a dark and stormy night," it also inverts the typical situation where a home symbolic of normalcy and rationality is intruded into by irrational forces. Here, it is the representative of the age of reason and American enlightenment, whose entering the humble abode of the firm believer in transcendence becomes aggressively avenged. "I seized it; I snapped it; I dashed it; I trod it; and dragging the dark lightning-king out of my door, flung his elbowed, copper sceptre after him," recounts the narrator (124). Yet, while the reader seems to be prompted to identify with the narrator, a didactic function hidden in the narrative creates a countering effect. A lot is learned on why copper as a better conductor than iron, and, therefore, is the appropriate choice for lightning rods (121), how one should "avoid pine-trees, high houses, lonely barns, upland pastures, running water, flocks of cattle and sheep, a crowd of men" during a storm (123), why it is advisable to stand in the middle of the room when lightning strikes (119). There are lessons to be learnt here, and it is the salesman the reader has to thank for them.

Incongruities are played out on three different levels in Melville's short story: first, the incongruity of style (everyday experience vs. hyperbolic, parodic stylization), secondly, the incongruity of genre expectations (irrational attack on rational lifeworlds vs. rational help brutally rejected), and thirdly on the autopoetic level by way of reflecting on literary epistemes. When carrying out comparative analyses between nineteenth-century classics and early twentieth-century Lovecraftian texts along with their contemporary memetic mutations, this paper relied on the presupposition that the formative years of creating a unique American identity made nineteenth-century American fiction particularly susceptible to genre variations: hoaxes, fantastic and proto-horror stories created by now highly canonized classics. Yet another reason is encoded in the history of American literature that has never ceased to exert its influence. The fact that puritan heritage (subversive in itself) has been paralleled with the ethics, core values, and rationalism of American enlightenment creates a doubled domain for the interpretation and creation of cultural artefacts. The recurrent waves of awakenings, transcendentalist and counter cultural movements have been accompanied in American cultural history by the legacy of the tenets originating in the Age of Reason. Melville's joke is on the incongruity of culture as well. It is as if Washington Irving were to chase Benjamin Franklin away out of whim— to utilize Rip Van Winkle as a meme. The uncertainty and hesitation between two epistemological domains in these co-present traditions is one of the causes of a peculiar sensibility towards the uncanny in American literature.

To return to Freud's essential essay for one last time, it is not uncanny that the Austrian founder of psychoanalysis should mention Mark Twain, whose *oeuvre* and life are full of humorously eerie stories with *Doppelgängers*, atemporal repetitions, chance events, and animistic superstitions. As quoted in books bearing such weird titles as *Unbelievable!: The Bizarre World of Coincidences*, or *Ghost Hunters: William James and the Search for Proof for Life After Death*. Twain predicted in 1909 his coming death foreshadowed by a most uncanny cosmic coincidence. "I came in with Halley's Comet in 1835. It is coming again next year, and I expect to go out with it. It will be the greatest disappointment of my life if I don't go out with Halley's Comet. The Almighty has said, no doubt: 'Now here are these two unaccountable freaks; they came in together, they must go out together'" (Heidon, Whitelaw 19). Together they went indeed.

Freud's reference is to Chapter XIII in Twain's travel novel (1880), *A Tramp Abroad* (49-53), where in a state between dream and consciousness the sleepy narrator crawls around the 'trauma' of an irritating mouse, almost as a parody of the queer atmosphere in Gilman's "The Yellow Wall-Paper." At one point, becoming utterly lost in circling around the ever missed encounter with the impertinent rodent finds its symbol in infinity mirrors: "If there had been only one mirror, it might possibly have helped to locate me; but there were two, and two were as bad as a thousand; besides these were on opposite sides of the room" (52). Knocking over pieces of furniture while crawling and creeping on his hands and knees, the narrator bumps into the same table, chair, and sofa coincidentally in compulsive repetition. His attempts to find his way in the darkness results in the multiplication of objects around him: "another chair," "another sofa" (53). This effect of doubling is resolved only by the collapse of uncanny darkness in radiating light. The narrator accidentally grasps a candlestick, knocks over a lamp, and wakes up his friend Harris, whose frantic shouting alarms the landlord, chambermaid, and guests in the house who come rushing in holding lanterns and candles, the light of which suddenly restores the singularity of objects and furniture. As a final punchline, the narrator reads his pedometer realizing that he had covered forty-seven miles while crawling and circling in the uncanny darkness of the room. Twain's piece is built exclusively on exaggeration and parody that creates a humorous effect of eerie incongruity.

Memes in genre transmutation

In her comprehensive essay "Horror and Humor" (1999), Noël Carrol summarizes the distinctive genre features of horredy with following statements:

> During the last decade or so, the subgenre of the horror-comedy has gained increasing prominence. Movies such as *Beetlejuice*, a triumph of this tendency, are predicated upon either getting us to laugh where we might ordinarily scream, or to scream where we might typically laugh, or to alternate between laughing and screaming throughout the duration of the film. One aim of this genre, it would appear, is to shift moods rapidly to turn from horror to humor, or vice versa, on a dime. (145)

A palpable trend not only in cinematography, but in fiction as well, for instance in *This Book Is Full of Spiders: Seriously, Dude, Don't Touch It* by James

Wong, or Joe Hill's *Horns*, horredy as a crossover seems thriving on the unexpected combination of the disproportionate juxtaposition of contradictory genre elements. As demonstrated in the outset of this section, incongruity as a formative aspect for both uncanny fiction and humor provides the intersecting domain for the merger of opposing aesthetic effects. The roller coaster experience in the alternate suturing of comic relief and the paranoia of horror elevates uncertainty and sustained hesitation to the level of genre expectations. This play on metapoetics is ever-present in *The Last Lovecraft: Relic of Cthulhu* (2009), a filmic adaptation loosely based on mythothemes in Cthulhu Mythos and "At the Mountains of Madness." The protagonists are Houellebecq's cosplaying Comic Con geeks, who suspectedly have never read a line by Lovecraft, yet memetic contamination through the intermediaries of comic books brings them to experience real-life contact with Lovecraftian monsters. With a twist in the plot, the male lead, Jeff Philips soon finds out that he is the genetic meme of Lovecraft himself, the last of his bloodline. Improbabilities in the plot-line, use of practical effects, plastic masks and low cost technical solutions, such as robotic tentacles of an unseen monster, along with metaplays on B-movie features are all utilized to create hesitancy between conflicting genre expectations towards comedy and/or horror. While the movie is crammed with graphic and gory violence, the audience has a chance to meet a fish-raped Captain Olaf, who keeps a Dunwich "merguy" as pet, with General Star-spawn, who calls the deep ones his pets, and with cult members, who are got even with a snorkel mask and fins. The final scene itself is centered around a meta-reference on all the meta-references sprayed on the movie. By this time the twenty-something kid-at-heart protagonists had managed to turn their weird adventures into a comic book, a copy of which one plum-faced ten-year-old fan asks them to sign. To pass the torch to the new generation, they tell him that the plot is based on a true story. The little boy rejects this idea as nonsense, but when he goes thorough the "real-life experience" of witnessing the start of the sequel when realizing that evil lives and has to be confronted at the mountains of madness, memetic contamination turns him into a believer, an enthusiast for what is still yet to come.

The single most successful direct adaptation of a Lovecraft story ever on the big screen must be Stuart Gordon's *Re-Animator* (1985), a gruesomely bizarre bonanza of sheer horror, which gained its memetic popularity for the exact opposite reason. Based on "Herbert West—Re-Animator" written for the humor magazine, *Home Brew* in 1922, the movie is acclaimed for its faithful recreation of the morbid atmosphere in the original story, although the adaptation features a damsel in distress as an addition to Lovecraft's exclusively male characters. One of the film's most repulsive, yet exhilaratingly funny scenes zooming in on Megan Halsey (1:11:00-1:12:07) enters dialogues twice in *American Beauty* (1999). First, the protagonist Lester Burnham meets the young Ricky Fitts, who works as a waiter at the party Lester is attending. They go out to the parking lot, where Ricky shares a joint with the middle-aged guest. The following scene ensues:

> LESTER BURNHAM. Did you ever see that movie where the body is walking around... carrying its own head, and then the head goes down on that babe?
> RICKY FITTS. Re-Animator! *[They burst out laughing.]* (0:32:22-31)

The second time Burnham, who is going through midlife crisis, decides to pick up on the guilty pleasure of his youth and visits Fitts to buy some weed. Too embarrassed to confront his new buddy directly with his real intention, he improvises a clandestine language:

> LESTER BURNHAM. I was thinking about the, uh... I was gonna... The movie we talked about.
> RICKY FITTS. Re-Animator.
> LESTER BURNHAM. Yeah!
> RICKY FITTS. You want to borrow it? Okay. It's up in my room. Come on. (45:29-48)

To date, "I want to borrow your copy of Re-animator" [sic] can be found as a slang term entry for the expression "I'd like to buy some pot" on Urban Dictionary. Memes are forever.

III. EVIL LIVES (AND IS CROSSING OVER)!

> "Eastern tales, introduced to European literature early in the eighteenth century through Galland's French translation of the inexhaustibly opulent *Arabian Nights*, had become a reigning fashion; being used both for allegory and for amusement. The sly humour which only the Eastern mind knows how to mix with weirdness had captivated a sophisticated generation, till Bagdad and Damascus names became as freely strewn through popular literature as dashing Italian and Spanish ones were soon to be."
>
> H. P. Lovecraft

The reemergence of the "weird" as "new weird" may cause a similar pandemonium for literary history in the future that the unfinished project of modernism created for postmodernism and post-postmodernism. Just as anything contemporary can be labeled as modern, due to its fundamentally memetic attribute, anything that is put in the category of "weird" must always be new. The performative act of memetic regeneration, application, borrowing, loaning, copying, stealing—as is illustrated by Poe's accusation of plagiarism leveled against Hawthorne's *Twice-Told Tale*—is not simply a characteristic feature of, or explanation for the protean nature inherent in genres of the uncanny, but its *raison d'être*. In the early nineteenth century the gothic imported from the British Isles fell on good ground in a cultural sphere still at its first stages of evolution, which was accelerated by a drive to become on a par with European predecessors and rivals. The formation of a unique American cultural identity, the subversive trait in puritan heritage, the co-presence of transcendentalist sensibilities and enlightened rationalism all were contributing factors in a cultural context that offered abundant examples for genre-crossings as consequence. These cultural impulses embedded in the heterogeneous historic position of the formative years and nativity of the emerging American literature not only created multifarious genre possibilities, but also shed light on the aporetic nature of genre formations as such while exposing a wide passage between high and low registers.

By identifying memes as the floating signifiers responsible for the continuous reiteration of genre formations without a detectable origin, this paper relied on Freud's findings in his authoritative essay on the nature of uncanny, entitled *Das Unheimliche* (1919). Freud determines six tropes that hint at, imply the inaccessible trauma encapsulated in the singularity as duration of utter uncertainty. Thus, the trauma of not being able to tell a story that is always hiding somewhere else is highlighted in this paper as the central tension and primal narrative force motivating and governing the uncanny poetics of weird tales. The six allegorizations of the uncanny identified in this work as an unceasing oscillation between dualities and triads were the following: (i) *Doppelgängers*; (ii) the Haunted House as an *unheimlich*, mirroring, *mise-en-abymic* place; (iii) the Automaton; (iv) Chance and Uncanny Coincidences; (v) the irrationality of signification in Madness and Atemporality; and finally (vi) Humor. In its dissolution into a triad, "[t]he double has become an object of terror" (Freud 143), where tropes of signification as the impossibility of a direct, denotative relation between sign and meaning create the six allegorizations of this uncanny hesitancy classified above.

Explorations into the nature of the Freudian *das Unheimliche*, genre constructions, atemporality associated with the irrationality of signification and repetitions displayed a similar asymmetrical, *mise-en-abymic* conformation represented in diagrams above that opens itself up for outward and inward mirroring. The presence of a category that contains itself as its own subcategory on one side of a subordinate polarity was disclosed in the structural conformation responsible for memetic regeneration. To justify the proposition that all six tropes of the uncanny have always been present as memes in American literature since the formative years of early nineteenth century through early twentieth century—when the label "weird" was coined—up to its return in the twenty-first century, comparative analyses of works by highly canonized classic authors were showcased and contrasted with the Lovecraftian *oeuvre* and its memetic transmutations in cinematography. A network of interwoven allegorizations of the uncanny was observed in the close readings, where the co-presence of several tropes could be detected in all works interpreted.

At its outset, this work endeavored to attempt at delineating discernable similarities in genre formations that are separated by more than a hundred years. The century through which the weird tale—but not its memes—seemed to be dormant is taken account of by Houellebecq in the following quote: "And no one, at least not for generations to come, will rebuild the faerie lace of the place of Irem" (63). Descriptions in *The Bas-Lag Cycle* by China Miéville might arguably be the case in point. From a historical, epistemological perspective, a resuscitated interest in metapoetics accompanied by a new propensity toward genre-crossings was needed for a new generation of writers to create masterpieces in the genre of the weird. For the weird as a tale never-to-be-told seems to be less about the plot line and more about its memetic elements creating an atmosphere of utter uncertainty. A new awareness of memes as formative components might be determined as cause for the proliferation of such genre constructions and labels as „steampunk," „fantastique," „bizarre," „science fantasy," „slipstream." There is one common denominator, though. Any story of the uncanny is always about the other story impossible to be told, it is about this ambience of impossibility and utter uncertainty brought about by memetic elements, which make the weird a passage way, a cross section among different genres and modes of artistic expression.

WORKS CITED

Alien. Directed by Ridley Scott, Twentieth Century Fox, 1979.
American Beauty. Directed by Sam Mendes, DreamWorks, 1999.
Bal, Mieke. *Narratology*. Toronto: University of Toronto Press, 1997.
Benczik Vera. "The City in Ruins: Post-9/11 Representations of Cataclysmic New York on Film." *Utopian Horizons: Ideology, Politics, Literature*, edited by Zsolt Czigányik, Budapest and New York: Central European University Press, 2017, 201-218.
Bennett, Andrew, and Nicholas Royle. "Pleasure." *Introduction to Literature, Theory and Criticism*, 3rd ed., London: Pearson Longman, 258–267.
Bierce, Ambrose. "An Occurrence at Owl Creek Bridge." *Tales of Soldiers and Civilians*, San Francisco: E. L. G. Steele, 1891, 21-39.
---. "Chickamauga." *Tales of Soldiers and Civilians*, San Francisco: E. L. G. Steele, 1891, 41-53.
---. "Haita the Shepherd." *Can Such Things Be?* Gloucester: Dodo Press, 2008, 149-154.
---. "The Death of Halpin Frayser." *Can Such Things Be?* Gloucester: Dodo Press, 2008, 1-15.
Blackmore, Susan. *The Meme Machine*. Oxford: Oxford University Press, 1999.
Blum, Deborah. *Ghost Hunters: William James and the Search for Proof for Life After Death*. New York: Penguin Books, 2006.
Bolyai János. *Appendix—The Theory of Space*, edited by Ferenc Kárteszi, Amsterdam: Elsevier, 1987.
Carrol, Noël. "Horror and Humor." *The Journal of Aesthetics and Art Criticism*, Vol. 57, No. 2, Aesthetics and Popular Culture (Spring, 1999), 145-160.
Carlin, Garry, and Nicola Allen. "Slime and Western Man: H. P. Lovecraft in the Time of Modernism." *New Critical Essay on H. P. Lovecraft*, edited by David Simmons, New York: Palgrave Macmillan, 2013, 73-91.
Chambers, Robert W. *The Hastur Cycle*. Chosium, 2006.
Clark, Michael. "Humor and Incongruity." *The Philosophy of Laughter and Humor*, edited by John Morreall, New York: State University of New York Press, 1987, 139–155.
Crompton, Jeremy. *Unbelievable!: The Bizarre World of Coincidences*. London: Michael O'Mara Books, 2013.
Dällenbach, Lucien. *The Mirror in the Text*. Translated by Jeremy Whitely and Emma Hughes. Oxford: Polity, 1989.
Dawkins, Richard. *The Selfish Gene*. Oxford: Oxford University Press, 1976.

deMan, Paul. "The Rhetoric of Temporality." *Blindness and Insight: Essays in the Rhetoric of Contemporary Criticism.* Minnesota: University of Minnesota Press, 1983, 187-229.

Derleth, August. *The Trail of Cthulhu.* London: Grafton, 1962.

Derrida, Jacques. *Spectres of Marx—The State of the Debt, Work of Mourning and the New International.* Translated by Peggy Kamuf. London: Routledge, 1994.

---, and Avital Ronell. "The Law of Genre." *Critical Inquiry*, Vol. 7, No. 1, On Narrative (Autumn, 1980), 55-81.

de Sitter, Willem. "The Size of the Universe" *Publications of The Astronomical Society Of The Pacific* Vol. XLIV. No. 258. San Francisco: California Academy of Sciences, 1932, 89-104.

Distin, Kate. *The Selfish Meme.* Cambridge: Cambridge University Press, 2005.

Dreams in the Witch House—a Lovecraftian Rock Opera. Platform West, LLC, 2013. CD. https://store.cdbaby.com/cd/dreamsinthewitchhouse (accessed Sept 29, 2017).

Foucault, Michel. *Madness and Civilization—A History of Insanity in the Age of Reason.* Translated by Richard Howard. New York: Vintage Books, 1988.

---. "Of Other Spaces, Heterotopias." *Architecture, Mouvement, Continuité* 5 (1984): 46-49.

---. "The Order of Discourse." Translated by Ian McLeod. *Untying the Text: A Post-Structuralist Reader*, edited by Robert Young, Boston: Routledge & Kegan Paul, 1981, 48-78.

Fraser, J.T. *The Genesis and Evolution of Time: A Critique of Interpretation in Physics.* Massachusetts: University of Massachusetts Press, 1982.

Freud, Sigmund. "The 'Uncanny'". Translated by James Strachey. *The Standard Edition of the Complete Psychological Works of Sigmund Freud, Volume XVII (1917-1919): An Infantile Neurosis and Other Works*, 217-256.

---. "The Uncanny (1919)." Translated by David Mcliontock. *The Uncanny*, edited by David Mcliontock, London: Penguin Classics, 2003, 121-162.

Gilman, Charlotte Perkins. "The Yellow Wall-Paper." *The Yellow Wall-Paper, Herland, and Selected Writings*, edited by Denise D. Knight, London: Penguin Books, 2009, 166-182.

Harvey, W. F. "August Heat." *When Churchyards Yawn*, edited by Niels W. Erickson, Bay Saint Louis: Couch Pumpkin Press, 2012, 234-239.

Hattenhauer, Darryl. *Shirley Jackson's American Gothic.* New York: State University of New York Press, 2003.

Heidon, Keith C., and Ian Whitelaw. *The Field Guide to Natural Wonders.* Hove: Quid Publishing, 2010.

Hill, Joe. *Horns.* New York: Harper, 2010.

Houellebecq, Michel. *H. P. Lovecraft: Against the World, Against Life.* Translated by Dorna Khazeni. San Francisco: Believer Books, 2005.

"I+Want+to+Borrow+Your+Copy+of+Re-Animator." *Urban Dictionary.* www.urbandictionary.com/define.php?term=I%2Bwant%2Bto%2Bbo rrow%2Byour%2Bcopy%2Bof%2BRe-animator (accessed Sept 01, 2017).

In the Mouth of Madness. Directed by John Carpenter, New Line Cinema, 1994.

Jackson, Shirley. "A Visit." *American Supernatural Tales*, edited by S.T. Joshi, New York: Penguin Books, 2007, 249-274.

James, Henry. "Sir Edmund Orme." *The Complete Stories 1884-1891*, edited by Henry James, et al., New York: Literary Classics of the United States, 1999, 851-881.

Jauss, Hans-Robert. *Toward an Aesthetic of Reception.* Translated by Timothy Bahti. Minnesota: University of Minnesota Press, 1982.

Jaynes, Julian. *The Origin of Consciousness in the Breakdown of the Bicameral Mind.* Boston: Houghton Mifflin, 1976.

Jentsch, Ernst. "On the psychology of the uncanny (1906)." *Angelaki*, vol. 2, no. 1, 1997, 7-16.

Joshi, Sunand Tryambak. *I Am Providence: The Life and Times of H.P. Lovecraft.* New York: Hippocampus Press, 2013.

Jung, Carl Gustav. *Synchronicity: An Acausal Connecting Principle.* Translated by R. F. C. Hull. Princeton and Oxford: Princeton University Press, 2010.

King, Stephen. "The Dune." *The Bazaar of Bad Dreams.* New York: Scribner, 2015, 81-96.

Lacan, Jacques. *The Seminar of Jacques Lacan (Book II: The Ego in Freud's Theory and in the Technique of Psychoanalysis).* Translated by Sylvana Tomaselli. Cambridge: Cambridge University Press, 1988.

---. *The Seminar of Jacques Lacan (Book X: Anxiety).* New York: Wiley, 2014.

---. *The Seminar of Jacques Lacan (Book XI: The Four Fundamental Concepts of Psycholanalysis).* New York: W. W. Norton, 1988.

Lovecraft, Howard Philip. "At the Mountains of Madness." *The Fiction: Complete and Unabridged.* New York: Barnes and Noble, 2008, 723-806.

---. "[In Defence of Dagon]: The Defence Remains Open!" (April 1921), *Collected Essays, Volume 5: Philosophy*, edited by S. T. Joshi, New York: Hippocampus Press, 2006, 54.

---. *Supernatural Horror in Literature.* Mineola: Dover Publications, 1973.

---. "The Call of Cthulhu." *The Fiction: Complete and Unabridged.* New York: Barnes and Noble, 2008, 355-379.

---. "The Case of Charles Dexter Ward." *The Fiction: Complete and Unabridged.* New York: Barnes and Noble, 2008, 490-593.

---. "The Dreams in the Witch House." *The Fiction: Complete and Unabridged.* New York: Barnes and Noble, 2008, 859-888.

---. "The Dunwich Horror." *The Fiction: Complete and Unabridged.* New York: Barnes and Noble, 2008, 633-667.

---. "The Outsider." *The Fiction: Complete and Unabridged.* New York: Barnes and Noble, 2008, 164-169.

---. "The Shadow Out of Time." *The Fiction: Complete and Unabridged.* New York: Barnes and Noble, 2008, 948-998.

---. "The Temple." *The Fiction: Complete and Unabridged.* New York: Barnes and Noble, 2008, 91-101.

---. "The Whisperer in Darkness." *The Fiction Complete and Unabridged.* New York: Barnes and Noble, 2008, 668-772.

---. "To Robert E. Howard." [29 Mar. 1933.] *Selected Letters*, edited by August Derleth and James Turner, vol. 4, Sauk City: Arkham House, 1976, 167-173.

Luckhurst, Roger. *Alien.* London: Palgrave Macmillan, 2014.

Lyotard, Jean-François. *Phenomenology.* Translated by Brian Beakley. New York: State University of New York Press, 1991.

Magny, Claude-Edmonde. *Histoire du roman français depuis 1918.* Éditions du Seuil, 1950.

Mangan, Bruce. "The Uncanny Valley as Fringe Experience." *Interaction Studies*, vol. 16, no. 2, 2015, 193–199.

Marshall, Kate. "The Old Weird." *Modernism/Modernity*, vol. 23, no. 2, Sept. 2016, 631–649.

Martin, Mike W. "Humor and the Aesthetic Enjoyment of Incongruities." *The Philosophy of Laughter and Humor*, edited by John Morreall, New York: State University of New York Press, 172–186.

Masters of Horror. Created by Mick Garris, IDT Entertainment, 2005-2007.

Melville, Herman. "The Lightning-Rod Man." *The Piazza Tales and Other Prose Pieces—Writings of Herman Melville; Vol. 9*, edited by Hayford Harrison et al., Evanston: Northwestern University Press, 1987, 118-124.

Michon, John A. "J. T. Fraser's 'Levels of Temporality' as Cognitive Representations." *The Study of Time V: Time, Science, and Society in China and the West*, edited by J. T. Fraser and N. Lawrence, Massachusetts: University of Massachusetts Press, 1986, 51-66.

Miéville, China. "Marxism and Fantasy: An Introduction." *Fantastic Literature: A Critical Reader*, edited by David Sandner, New York: Praeger, 2004, 334–344.

---. *The City & The City.* London: Pan Books, 2009.

---. "Weird Fiction." *The Routledge Companion to Science Fiction*, edited by Mark Bould, London: Routledge, 2009, 510-517.

Mills, Alice. *Seriously Weird: Papers on the Grotesque.* New York: P. Lang, 1999.

Mitchell, Charles P. *The Complete H. P. Lovecraft Filmography.* Westport: Greenwood Press, 2001.

Morreall, John. "A New Theory of Laughter." *The Philosophy of Laughter and Humor*, edited by John Morreall, New York: State University of New York Press, 128–138.

Noys, Benjamin, and Timothy S. Murphy. "Old and New Weird." *Genre*, vol. 49, no. 2, July 2016, 117-134.
Petersen, Sandy, and Lynn Willis. *Horror Roleplaying—Call of Cthulhu*. Hayward: Chaosium, 1999.
Poe, Edgar Allan. *The Works of Edgar Allan Poe. VOl 1.*, edited by John H. Ingram, London: A. & C. Black, SohoSquare, 1899.
Prékopa András, and Molnár Emil (Eds.). *Non-Eucledian Geometries—János Bolyai Memorial Volume*. New York: Springer, 2006.
Prince of Darkness. Directed by John Carpenter, Alive Films, 1987.
Rank, Otto. *[der Doppelgänger.] The Double— a Psychoanalytic Study*. Translated and edited by Harry Tucker Jr., Chapel Hill: University of North Carolina Press, 1971.
Re-Animator. Directed by Stuart Gordon, Empire Pictures, 1985.
Schelling, Friedrich Wilhelm Joseph. *Philosophie der Mythologie* (1835). München: Fink, 1996.
Smith, Clark Ashton. "The Tale of Satampra Zeiros." *Lost World*. University of Nebraska Press, 2006, 3-17.
Spaulding, Todd. "The Emerge(d)Nt Weird Tale: A Genre Study." *Studies in the Fantastic*, vol. 3, 2015, 76–99.
The Encyclopedia of The Gothic, edited by William Hughes, David Punter, & Andrew Smith. Oxford: Wiley-Blackwell, 2013.
The Haunted Palace. Directed by Roger Corman, Alta Vista Productions, 1963.
The Last Lovecraft: Relic of Cthulhu. Directed by Henry Shaine, Outlaw Films, 2009.
The Mist. Directed by Frank Darabont, Dimension Films, 2007.
Todorov, Tzvetan. *The Fantastic: A Structural Approach to a Literary Genre 1970*. Translated by Richard Howard. Ithaca: Cornell University Press, 1975.
Twain, Mark. *A Tramp Abroad*. Mineola: Dover Publications, 2002, 49-53.
Twin Peaks. Created by Mark Frost and David Lynch. Lynch/Frost Productions, 2017.
Vandeermeer, Ann, and Jeff Vandermeer. *The New Weird*. San Francisco: Tachyon Publications, 2008.
Wong, James. *This Book Is Full of Spiders: Seriously, Dude, Don't Touch It*. New York: Thomas Dunne Books, 2012.

www.ingramcontent.com/pod-product-compliance
Lightning Source LLC
Chambersburg PA
CBHW061343040426
42444CB00011B/3065